What Others Are Saying About
Typical Thoughts, Triumphant Results!

"Dr. Fitzgerald is a miracle worker, this process works! By replacing self-defeating thoughts and attitudes, and tapping into your power, you can achieve extraordinary results."
Carole Ann Heller, *Henry Ford Health Care, Detroit, MI*

"Redefines your thinking to find both personal and professional potential. Essential information for managers who want to help employees maximize their success."
Jan Hydruzuiko, *Training Manager, Sandy Corporation, Detroit, MI*

"Inspires, entertains and promotes action. The visualization scripts make it easy for anyone to make positive changes in their life."
Karen Elaine Ervin, *The Kee to Speaking Success, Atlanta, Ga.*

" ... get ready to change your life forever...a must read for all seeking the best in themselves."
 Darryl Hold, *On-Line Seminars, Waleska, Ga*

" ... teaches you how to use thoughts, behaviors, actions and visualization to achieve triumphant success."
George Austin, *Associate Dean, DeVry Institute of Technology*

"As a therapist, I know that many people learn a new skill and relapse within 10 –14 days, this book helps us transcend these hurdles."
 Sharon Lotosky, *Life Solutions, Warren, Michigan*

"This book teaches valuable tools for successfully achieving both business and personal goals. A must read for anyone who is serious about empowering themselves to reach their fullest potential."
 Marilyn Young, *Director of Administrative Services,*
 San Diego County Water Authority

"Skilled trades have known for some time that visualization works. This book advances the concepts of how to use visualization as a training tool."
 Virgil Norgrove, *Technical Training Coordinator, Visteon Corporation*

Typical Thoughts
Triumphant Results
A Five-Step Strategy For Mastering Your Potential!

F.A.C.T. Publication
Georgia

Typical Thoughts
Triumphant Results
A Five-Step Strategy For Mastering Your Potential!

Liv Fitzgerald, Ph.D.

Published by:
F.A.C.T.
P.O. Box 6124
Marietta, GA 30062
F.A.C.T.S@att.net

Publisher's Cataloging-in-Publication
(Provided by Quality Books, Inc.)

Fitzgerald, Liv.
    Typical thoughts triumphant results : a five-step strategy for mastering your potential! / author, Liv Fitzgerald ; editors, Laurie Knox and Mimi Taylor ; cover, Bill Niesen. -- 1st ed.
    p. cm.
    Includes bibliographical references.
    LCCN 2001126625
    ISBN 0-9-712544-0-0

    1. Success--Psychological aspects. 2. Visualization. 3. Communication. I. Title.

BF637.S8F58 2001   158
                  QB101-700900

Warning-Disclaimer

This book is designed to educate and offer suggestions for achieving personal and business success with communication and visualization.

It is sold with the understanding that the publisher and author are not engaged in rendering professional services. If professional service or advice is required, the services of a competent professional should be sought. Additionally, before beginning any weight loss or exercise programs, please consult a physician.

There was no intent to reprint all of the information that is available to authors, publishers or the public, but instead to offer another option that may complement other texts. I urge you to read all available material, learn as much as possible about achieving personal and business success with communication and visualization, and tailor the information to your needs.

Every effort has been made to make this book as complete and accurate as possible. However, there may be mistakes, both typographical and in content. Therefore, use the information as a general guide not as an ultimate source of achieving personal success. Furthermore, this information is only up to the copyright date.

The author/publisher shall have neither liability nor responsibility to any person or entity with respect for loss or damage caused, or alleged to have been caused, directly or indirectly, by the information contained in this book.

If you do not wish to be bound by the above, please contact the author/publisher/ for a full refund.

About The Author

Liv Fitzgerald, Ph.D., is a nationally renowned speaker, trainer and consultant. She has helped thousands of people overcome their obstacles to achieve personal and business success.

Dr. Fitzgerald has designed organizational training programs, and trained executives and employees at Federal Reserve Bank, GMAC Management Training, and Ford Motor Company. She taught communication classes at Georgia State University and Kennesaw University.

After studying communication and visualization for her doctoral dissertation, Fitzgerald continues researching and combining these powerful techniques. Her mission is to help you achieve results that, until now, may have seemed insurmountable. "The miracle worker," as she has often been called, refers to the power she brings out in you.

Today, she is the president of Fitzgerald Applied Communication Training in Marietta, Georgia. Her books, training and speaking topics offer her audience the power to stretch beyond their self-imposed boundaries.

Now, she is revealing these techniques to you. You can use the pre-designed visualization scripts to help you achieve your desired results, or design your own scripts by following the information in this book.

Contents

This book is dedicated to my parents who instilled

a belief that I could achieve anything I desired,

to my friend Bill, his patience and help will be

remembered for a lifetime, and

to my sons, Brian and Keith, their energy and

perseverance in each endeavor is an eloquent reminder of

the spectacular gift we have each been given ...

life.

Typical Thoughts, Triumphant Results
A Five-Step Strategy For Mastering Your Potential!

Introduction

I met Emma-May in a speech class I was instructing. She was 80 years old. When I asked why she was taking a college class she said, "I've been a nurse for fifty years and frankly I'm sick of it. I'm changing careers. I'm going into business administration."

Emma-May is my inspiration. Nothing stopped this lady from experiencing her possibilities. The day you begin to read this book is the day a world of possibilities will begin opening up for you too. Today you start on the journey of learning how to control your destiny. It can happen if you are willing to apply the strategies taught in this book. You will gain the motivation to make positive changes in your life. You will decide the route your life will take, and you will achieve it.

Although it is difficult for some people to believe, most limitations are self-imposed. That is actually good news. It's good news because when we put limitations upon ourselves, logically, we can eliminate them by ourselves. As adults, we make the final decision about what we will do, when we will do it, how we will do it, and if we feel like doing it at all. Even when we allow someone else to decide for us, the decision to give control of our lives to someone else is our own. Creating a mindset for success means finding out what makes you happy and fulfilled, and going after it.

We all have self-imposed limits, and some are even realistic. It is realistic to eat smaller portions if you want to maintain your weight, it's realistic to exercise if you want to be healthy and in good shape. Even society imposes limits. These are designed to keep us from harming ourselves or others, such as seat belt laws, traffic lights and limits on how fast we can drive cars, and limits on alcohol consumption, to name a few. To get along better in life we need realistic boundaries; the unrealistic boundaries and beliefs are the ones we want to overcome.

My first notable unrealistic belief was that I was not smart enough to go to college. I realized that when I got a "D" in school, my parents did not reprimand me. Perhaps my parents felt "D" work was all I was capable of accomplishing. So all I got were D's from that point on. Hence the belief that I was not very smart. It was years before I was able to dispel this belief by enrolling in one college class and receiving my first "A." I had proven the non-existence of one unrealistic belief. That college class began my educational quest. It also began my search for new ways to achieve success by confronting, challenging, and overcoming self-imposed, destructive beliefs.

Each of us has the capability of creating the

life that we desire. You may not believe this yet, but keep reading. Eventually, you will go beyond your current beliefs, and you will reach a new plateau. You will reach a place in your mind that has no doubts, only a trust and knowing that what you desire will happen.

Perhaps you're thinking you have some unique problem that cannot be overcome. The limits and boundaries we place on ourselves are very individualized; however, people who produce desirable results have several common characteristics. This book explores the common characteristics needed to achieve your desires. Although we each have the capacity to produce greatness for ourselves, nobody says we have to do it alone. We can learn the characteristics others have used to produce greatness. We often think that people who have "made it" in life have special advantages, when in truth, they are just like everybody else with one major difference: they have learned to create a mindset that produces positive results. You can learn this too. One of those characteristics is effective communication.

"Effective communication" is often cited when people are asked what they need in order to be more successful in their endeavors. I agree, and apparently so does the research. It's ironic that we learn how to do just about everything in school except how to communicate effectively. We learn communication from our parents who usually have had no formal training in communication and consequently, inadequate communication skills are handed down from generation to generation. Yet we need effective communication in our personal lives. It is through communication that we gain and receive the information needed for success. Communication helps us create what we desire in our lives, it helps us achieve our dreams, it helps us create healthy relationships with spouses, children, co-workers and customers, yet more and more we are failing in this endeavor. This is especially unfortunate because ineffective communication is a problem that can be remedied.

Many people feel that communication is manipulative, and it is! The Merriam-Webster dictionary says to manipulate is to manage skillfully. Communication helps us manage our lives skillfully. When we're skilled in communication, we have fewer misunderstandings, we make fewer mistakes, and we deal with disagreements more effectively. Perfecting our communication is essential for achieving success.

While communication is considered an area that needs improvement, most people don't seem to think that their own communication needs adjustment. Everybody else needs help! We expect others to change, when in reality, the only person you can change is *"you."*

Wouldn't it be wonderful, though, if we really could make the whole world change for us? The catch is that when we blame others, we are in effect giving up control over our own lives; we are implying that there is nothing we can do ourselves to improve a bad situation. We could blame others for poor listening habits instead of finding a better way to express ourselves. We could blame our spouses, friends, and co-workers for not understanding our point of view, when in reality we have not tried to understand their point of view. We hold others responsible when our dreams fail, when in reality we can create our own dreams. The common thread here is the belief that our lives are limited by outside forces.

We are more objective in accepting that we need change in other areas of our lives. We know when we need to lose weight, so we diet or exercise, or stay overweight; when we want to look younger we use cosmetics, teeth whiteners and hair dye; but when we are not getting what we desire in our life, we expect others to change. Why not expect the entire world to get fat so we don't seem so overweight? Why not expect others to make themselves look older so we can feel young again? Because trying to change the entire world is an unrealistic and tedious undertaking, which is why this book looks at changes the individual can make to attain personal success. It's quicker and easier to change ourselves than to try and change everyone else.

The areas of communication this book helps you change in order to master your potential are your thoughts, behaviors, and developing an action plan. Simply put, when your thoughts and behaviors are congruent, when you follow an action plan, achieving your outcomes is as natural as breathing.

The characteristic needed to unleash your power is being able to visualize your desires. It was during my Ph.D. program that I discovered visualization. But until I began Fitzgerald Applied Communication Training seminars, I did not truly see what a powerful tool visualization is for achieving greatness in our lives. In the seminars, training is conducted on both a conscious and a subconscious level. On the conscious level, the approach employs lecture, role-play, creative thinking, discussion, behavioral modeling, and actual practice. On the subconscious level, the communication tool is visualization. I've had many opportunities to use these training techniques and observe their benefits. Visualization has some unique qualities that other learning techniques lack. First, visualization is a mental practice, a powerful tool that aligns the conscious and subconscious minds. We can think of the conscious and subconscious as our "two selves." Unfortunately, these "two selves" work under two different sets of rules: the conscious mind is critical, while the subconscious mind is open and accepting of what it learns. When we can get both "selves" to work as a contiguous unit, instead of separately, the possibilities for expanding and embellishing our lives are limitless. Second, visualization is like having an arbitrator helping the conscious and subconscious get along. When messages enter our mind, the arbitrator withholds critical judgements from the conscious mind and sends the positive messages to the subconscious. In other words, when the conscious mind learns a new technique, it often becomes critical, thinking, "that will never work." Visualization impedes the flow of critical thought from the conscious mind and allows the subconscious to simply accept what it learns. When criticism is suspended, you can learn faster and achieve a stronger transfer of skills. Visualization is highly effective in influencing the performance of successful outcomes. For example, if you wanted to stop smoking, your conscious mind might say, "I've tried that, it's too hard." With visualization, the conscious mind is not given the opportunity to be critical, and the subconscious mind can go to work acting on the information it receives. In the subconscious, there is no room for doubt; the subconscious believes you can successfully achieve anything you desire. And as long as you can suspend judgements from the conscious mind, anything is possible.

Does visualization work? Thirty years of research indicates it does. Beginning with an article in Golf Digest, Wells (1962) claimed that visualization produced positive thoughts, built confidence, and enabled athletes to feel more relaxed. With visualization, Wells said that one could actually produce a better golf swing without even picking up a golf club and swinging.

In 1972, an observational study was conducted with athletes using visualization to train for the winter Olympics. The athletes produced positive results and used techniques during the actual activity that had only been practiced with the visualization.

Today, most of visualization research is concentrated in the areas of sport psychology, education and communication. While many researchers have discovered visualization's virtues, no one, as yet, can explain why it works. Some researchers report positive results with visualization while other researchers doubt its capabilities. As one researcher writes, while scientific research remains inconclusive, even those who question the effects of visualization acknowledge that the mind is complex and obviously capable of more than we understand.

Although visualization is out of the mainstream of research, being open to new ideas is often what creates greatness. I ask only that you be open to the possibility that visualization may create greatness in your life. All things are possible when you are open to learning and trying something new. It is in this spirit of investigation that I offer you this book.

My research includes years of observation and interviews conducted in training seminars, as well as a formal study of visualization for my doctoral dissertation. In this study, visualization was applied to a real life setting, rather than a lab study. Visualization was used as a training tool to teach team development. Even the most resistant members of the teams, members who believed visualization would not be effective for them, or members who said they could not mentally visualize pictures, improved their performance with visualization. Additionally, members reported continued future use of the techniques taught in the seminar throughout the following year. For these people, visualization was an effective tool for learning new skills and for communicating effectively with other team members.

This book focuses on you as the sender and receiver of communication. You will learn how to use visualization as a communication tool to gain control over what happens in your life. You'll be offered practical ways to attain personal success. You'll learn to change the things you're unhappy with and enhance the areas of your life that are working well. If you follow the exercises, you'll learn how to achieve personal success. You can acquire new skills or make significant improvements in your ability to achieve success by using the methods discussed. This book offers you a step-by-step guide to manage your communication skillfully, with visualization.

My years as an organizational trainer have enabled me to create the training exercises that make this book unique. You are offered a hands-on-training program to help you determine your personal strategies, make changes, and achieve positive results! This book puts the focus on you, meaning that you'll be asked to think and decide if your communication patterns and style need revision. If you want to improve your communication and achieve desirable results, work through this book, step by step. Each chapter in this book builds upon the previous chapter offering techniques and exercises to help you achieve your desired results. Work on the exercises, then try them in your life. I believe you'll be pleased with the end results.

The chapters contain actual stories of people who overcame obstacles in their lives. People who often knew what to do or say, but couldn't put it into action; people who wanted to lose weight, stop smoking, begin an exercise program, reduce stress, achieve stronger relationships, or achieve their dreams, but knew that their communication styles were hindering their success. Good communication is invaluable for friends who want to get along better with each other, and for anyone striving to achieve their dreams. All these people learned techniques that changed their lives. Each chapter is designed to help you determine where you've self-imposed unrealistic boundaries, to help you decide what you want, and then to take the corrective action necessary to achieve it.

This book is organized into two sections:

Section One: *The Communication Phase* helps you develop thoughts, behaviors, and an action plan for success. Section one helps you take charge of your life.

Section Two: *The Visualization Phase* offers visualization scripts for personal use. There are visualization scripts to help you lose weight, stop smoking, enjoy exercising, reduce stress and strengthen your personal relationships. The maintenance scripts insure your success. Additionally, you will learn how to design your own visualization script for specific needs that may not be covered in this book. After reading this book you'll be able to make adjustments, if needed, in each of these areas to get what you desire in life. This book is written for those who are interested in self-improvement. It is up to you to define success. It is up to you to apply the techniques discussed; it is up to you to learn from this book and decide to make the changes that best suit you.

Imagine standing on the shore of your own island watching the beautiful waves. Now imagine you're surfing, riding high on the crest of a wave. If you hit a rough spot and fall, you'll soon know what to do to get back on top. It takes a little practice, a little patience, but with a little time, it works!

If you positively knew you would succeed, what would you be doing today

Liv Fitzgerald

Chapter One

Questions Precede Change

When I was a kid, my father would take the wheels off my bicycle in the winter and store them in the basement; the frame was stored in the backyard shed. When I had children, I followed the same wintertime routine with their bikes. When my sons, Brian and Keith, were capable of removing the wheels themselves, I delegated the responsibility. Along with the delegation was the question, "Why do we have to take the wheels off our bikes, Mom?"

I had assumed the cold Michigan winters had an adverse effect on bike tires, but my sons decided to ask their grandfather why this tradition began. Grandpa said, "I took the wheels off the bike because that was the only way the bike would fit into my shed."

Perhaps it is time to start questioning the way you have always done things.

Once we begin to question, we are open to change. The process of questioning the "givens" in our lives and becoming open to change is the first strategy needed for attaining what you desire in your life.

Based on my father's explanation, I will never take wheels off a bike again! This is one of those changes that was easy to incorporate into my life. Not all changes are so easy. If you live in an area that recently had to start dialing an area code along with the phone number, how often did you end up with a message "We're sorry, when placing a local call it is now necessary to dial an area code and a 7-digit number; please hang up and redial using a complete ten digit number."

How long did it take before you remembered to dial the area code before the phone number? Most of us were probably sick of hearing the operator long before the change became routine. Research indicates it takes approximately 21 days to change a habit. Change is often difficult because, like it or not, we are creatures of habit.

One of my mother's habits was refusing to put her glasses on when she was driving. She seemed to do okay until it was time to park. She kept parking her car on the neighbor's car bumper, and she preferred to blame our neighbor for purchasing a car with a protruding bumper.

"Maybe you should start wearing those glasses," I remember saying. "You've hit that car four times." Mom insisted that once she started relying on glasses, she would never be able to go without them. We could only hope.

It is much easier to look at our parents and friends and see that they have become creatures of habit. But we are all creatures of habit; the only difference is that our own habits are often performed unconsciously.

I never realized I was a creature of habit until my son, Keith, reminded me of a sore throat remedy I have used for forty years. This remedy was handed down from my grandmother, who got it from her mother. If I get a sore throat I put a mentholated rub on my throat and keep my throat wrapped until the sore throat disappears. For forty years, even though the sore throat disappeared, I always ended up with laryngitis. Sometimes it's tough to change even when we're not getting good results. And sometimes these poor results go on for generations!

Think about it, a lot of what you do today is what you learned from your parents. You've learned how and when and what to eat from your parents. You've probably learned how to handle stress from your parents too, which could include nail biting, lateness, overeating, or the use of alcohol and cigarettes, to name a few ineffective but popular stress reducers. It's tough to break habits that have been developing for years, and given the way habits are handed down through families, even centuries!

Habits are not the only emotional inheritance our parents give us. Their hopes and dreams often become ours too. My son, Brian, swears he would never have gone to college if I had not pushed him. I don't regret pushing this upon him. Yet research indicates that most college students graduate at 24 years old, and at 25 they finally decide what they would have liked to study in college. As much as I tried not to influence

Brian on what to study in college, when he reached 170 credits, (he needed 120 to graduate) I started pushing him to complete a degree. He did, and now he's considering returning to college to study what interests him.

We also learn boundaries and fears from our parents. When I was in my twenties, a neighborhood friend, Bob, was building his own house. Bob was not a builder; he was a firefighter and had learned from a friend how to subcontract a house. Bob agreed to teach my husband, Paul, and me how to subcontract a house. In fact, Bob convinced us that we could build the entire house for the $9,000.00 we had saved (it was 1970). A three-bedroom 1,000 square foot home could be purchased for approximately $30,000 in Michigan at this time. My father, on the other hand, was convinced that building was a bad idea, that Paul and I would lose all we had saved. "You don't know anything about building," Dad said. He was right, but Paul and I didn't let ignorance stop us. We worked with Bob, learned from Bob, and we built the house for $13,000. It was more than Bob estimated, but two kids in their twenties had a house paid for because we took a chance; we didn't allow my father's concerns to stop us, nor did we hold ourselves back. My father was now convinced that building was a good idea. Dad built a house the following year.

Kids seem to instinctively know that holding back is too much work, which is the attitude that often gets teenagers into trouble. It is during these teenage years that learning to be mature becomes associated with learning to delay gratification. Unfortunately, many adults take delayed gratification to an extreme and give up on their dreams. Many adults appear to find an area of comfort and remain in that zone whether they are happy or not. You would think we would only hold back on things that we fear; yet we often hold back in small ways, too. I know a lady who went to the same grocery store for years, despite the fact that her husband had taken a new job that relocated the family forty miles from the grocery store. "I know where to find what I need," she rationalized. I know a gentleman who went to the same hairdresser for years, although he was never satisfied with his haircuts. When I asked why he didn't try a new hairdresser he said, "at least I know how my hair will turn out with my current hairdresser."

In order to get what you desire in your life, you may want to start questioning what is not working. You may find it is time to stretch beyond your comfort zone. One thing is for sure, *"If you stay right where you are, nothing will change."*

Comfort Zone List

Let's take a look at your comfort zone. Using a 100-point scale, list the things you are comfortable doing in the first 20 points. These will probably be things you do on a daily or weekly basis such as grocery shopping, changing the car oil, or cooking an intimate dinner for two. Perhaps going out to dinner alone would be a bit more uncomfortable, and would fall in the 20-40 points. Between 40 and 60 points might be starting a new job. What would fall between 60-80 points? Where would public speaking fall?

Moving? Going back to school? Going after your biggest dream? Unattained goal? The 90 -100 ranges are probably your greatest fears or intimidations.

List something in each area that you would like to try also, but that you have not yet found the courage for. Maybe you've never tried roller-skating and you think it falls in the 1-20 zone. Maybe you already own a business but you want to try a new marketing plan, or you want to introduce a new product. If you could do anything you wanted, what would that be? Where would it fit on your list?

Comfort Zone List

Zone One - 20/ Most Comfortable

1	11
2	12
3	13
4	14
5	15
6	16
7	17
8	18
9	19
10	20

Zone 21-40/Somewhat Intimidating

21	31
22	32
23	33
24	34
25	35
26	36
27	37
28	38
29	39
30	40

Zone 41-60/ Even More Intimidating

41	51
42	52
43	53
44	54
45	55
46	56
47	57
48	58
49	59
50	60

Zone 61-80/ Fearful

61	71
62	72
63	73
64	74
65	75
66	76
67	77
68	78
69	79
70	80

Zone 81-100 /Greatest Fears or Challenges

81	91
82	92
83	93
84	94
85	95
86	96
87	97
88	98
89	99
90	100

The zone you feel the most comfortable in should be 1-20. The idea is to add items to each zone that you would like to try, and then to gradually try them. Take one zone a week, and work up to the greatest fear zone. An interesting thing happens when you leave your comfort zone: at first you feel uncomfortable, but once you've been in a different zone for a bit, your comfort zone stretches. For example, if you try something in the 60-80 zone, your normal comfort zone begins to expand. Normal will no longer be 20; instead, you'll feel comfortable somewhere between 20 and 60. You have stretched. The items in the 20-40 zone probably won't look so difficult once you have been in the 60-80 zone.

Think of this stretching process like blowing up a balloon. The balloon starts out taut, but after you've blown it up a few times, and released the air, it becomes more flexible. At any rate, the balloon never returns to its original position after it has been stretched. Neither will you!

It takes much more energy to stay taut. Tighten your arm muscles and try to remain that way for five minutes. It is much easier to relax your muscles than hold them taut. Any time you are holding back on a thought or behavior, you are also in a taut position. Head muscles that tighten become a headache. When we finally let go of a taut position and go after what we want, we often express our relief by saying, "it feels like a weight was lifted off my shoulders." This describes the muscles finally relaxing in our shoulders. It eases the tension to go after what we want rather than to hold back.

Jake, a friend of mine, finally returned to college after years of procrastination. He described going after his desire like this, "Once I made the decision to go back to college, I felt like getting up in the morning again. I had something to live for.

My zest for life returned. It's as though my entire body relaxed with that decision to return to school, not just to say I wanted to go to school, but to do it. I used to think about returning to school and I'd immediately start rationalizing why I couldn't do it, and almost as immediately I could feel my chest tighten up, and a sick feeling in the pit of my stomach. Getting up each day for a job I disliked increased my symptoms. I found myself taking a lot of time off work. I missed 12 days of work last year. Since the day I signed up for classes (more than one year ago), I have not been sick one day."

The difference all comes down to how we communicate with ourselves. Our thoughts and our behaviors, when congruent, are capable of achieving a specific action. That action could be to our benefit or to our dismay. I had a student, Mindy, who hated taking tests. She not only told herself she was a poor test taker but on the day of the test her body became so tense that she could not think. As a result, she failed her tests. Mindy's thoughts and behaviors were congruent, and she was certainly achieving a specific action, but she was not achieving a desirable result.

On the other hand is my college friend, Dennis. Dennis and I were working on our Ph.D. at the same time. Ten years ago Dennis was a drinking alcoholic living on the streets in Detroit.

"I watched how people survived on the streets," Dennis said. "Being a quick learner, I was able to beg for food, money, a bottle, and to find a warm place to sleep in a matter of days, despite being drunk." He survived on the streets for three years. One day Dennis started talking to a man who had also once lived on the streets but had returned to society. The man proudly described his job, and his income. He talked about how he received a college degree, and started a family. Dennis started questioning his own existence and decided he wanted a change in his life. From living on the streets to earning a Ph.D. is certainly a change. In order to make this change, Dennis had to visualize it as a real possibility.

Visualization helps people communicate in a manner that achieves desirable results, and offers the potential for achieving success. Despite decisions, tests, and adversities to overcome throughout our lives, some people have a plan, or learn one, that puts them on top every time. Have you ever questioned how they do this? How is it that some people are born with numerous advantages, yet somehow the decisions they make are marked with tragic endings? How is it that someone like Dennis, with seemingly no advantages, pulled himself up from the dredges and landed on top? How is it someone born into an impoverished life, or a life with physical defects, like Stevie Wonder, can take the experience and make the most of it? The difference is in how we communicate to ourselves. Visualization offers a plan to optimize our communication and achieve a mindset that creates success.

Visualization

"Beware!" You will get what you desire if you are willing to go after it. You will learn to rid yourself of any obstacles that hold you back. I promise!

Can you imagine what your life would be like if it had no obstacles? Imagine that for a moment. Where would you be? Guess what? You don't have to live with bounds. If you can visualize what you desire, whatever it is, you can achieve it through visualization. Visualization works!

Questioning your current existence often brings concerns and self-doubt. However, visualization offers an effective technique to help you achieve your desires. You have to make a choice to use visualization, and to practice visualization to achieve and maintain your goals.

What is Visualization?

Visualization is a mental practice, a form of focused attention. It creates a *positive* mental attitude and allows you to practice behaviors that lead to achieving the desired goal. Instead of thinking of all that could go wrong in a goal endeavor, your imagination creates a detailed, positive and vivid mental image of successful goal completion. It is a voluntary achievement of a state of mind that can help you modify thoughts and behaviors. To progress in just about any endeavor, you must first decide that you want it, and next you must decide that you can achieve it. Then you must imagine yourself taking the steps to complete your task successfully. This book takes you through the steps to complete your task successfully and achieve what you desire.

Visualization has been used successfully in sports programs for years. Every top athlete knows that success depends on mental attitude and concentration as much as on physical ability. Sports psychologists say that 80-85 percent of top athletes use positive imagery (visualization) in their training. Basketball players, dart-throwers, runners, golfers and Olympic athletes have improved their attitudes through visualization. By imaging themselves successfully completing tasks, athletes have enhanced their performance. Tennis players Chris Evert and Martina Navratilova, figure skaters Brian Boitano and Kristi Yamaguchi and gymnast Mary Lou Retton have all used visualization.

Retton said, "Before I dropped off to sleep inside the Olympic Village, I did what I always do before a major competition -- mind scripted it completely. I mentally ran through each routine, every move, imagining everything was done perfectly" (McGarvey, 1990).

Psychologists believe that we act as the persons we "see" ourselves to be. If you tell yourself, or others, "I can't ask for a promotion," or "I can't increase my income," you can't! No amount of encouragement or practice will help you achieve your desires as long as deep inside, you believe you cannot achieve your goals. Visualization allows us to mentally practice using behaviors that produce positive mental change; ultimately it allows us to create our own success.

With the help of visualization, I stated jogging when I turned 45 years old, and I lost ten pounds. I'd like to preface this by stating I hated jogging. I had tried jogging on several previous occasions and given up each time. Generating positive mental images helped me learn to enjoy jogging. I actually learned to enjoy something I believed I hated.

While the academic world is still trying to understand why visualization works, we do know something about how it works. These are the essential steps: 1) remove the fears and misconceptions about visualization by learning what it is, 2) enter a relaxed, but alert state to begin the visualization exercise, 3) create images to perform the task successfully, 4) rehearse the physical activity by imagining yourself performing the activity and feeling your body carrying out the desired action, 5) mentally rehearse the desired activity in detail, such as how to throw a ball, how to hold a dart, how to build positive thoughts and confidence.

Mental practice helps you become consistent, not necessarily perfect. If you mess up, you simply rehearse the desired outcome mentally again so that when the actual performance takes place, it will take less time to perfect the skill than would be possible with no mental rehearsal at all (Ryans & Simons, 1982).

Sport psychologists, educators, and communication experts have all shown interest in visualization, each with a different focus. Sport psychologists use visualization to rehearse physical activity and aid in positive thinking. Educators add cognitive skills to visualization's virtues. They credit visualization as an aid in learning, memory, and reducing anxiety to help people perform better: learners can generate their own visual representation to enhance learning and recall. In an experimental study by Rasco, Tennyson & Boutwell (1975), college students were asked to read an all verbal passage. Students who were asked to create their own mental images of the verbal passage had better recall than those in read-only groups and those in a group who read the passage and viewed supplemental pictures. Education scholars are becoming increasingly interested in visualization as a study strategy since even students who claim to be poor at visualizing are able to enhance learning and memory by using it. Communication experts combine the strategies of sport psychology and education. Communication experts use visualization to help us improve how we talk to ourselves (our intrapersonal patterns) and, how we adapt behaviors. Used correctly, visualization can help us adjust our communication patterns to achieve desired outcomes.

When I interviewed Jake regarding his plans to return to school, he had a very negative thought pattern. He knew exactly why he should not return to school: 1) it would cost too much money, 2) it would take time from his family, 3) he couldn't afford to reduce his work hours to part-time so it would double the time for him to complete his education. When Jake discussed his thoughts, his body language was sullen, he slumped in his chair, he hung his head as if he were ashamed, he looked depressed. Jake was asked to begin picturing himself actually going to college, and to think about how good it would feel to follow his dream. He was then asked to picture himself with his college degree and the job of his dreams, and to imagine how good it would feel to get up every day in that new life. Jake's entire body language changed as he visualized a change in his thought process. Suddenly he held his head high, he was smiling, his shoulders and back lifted. Changing both his thoughts and his behaviors created a new outlook.

For others, visualizing a change in behavior alone can affect a positive change. Try this: smile, widen your eyes, lift your eyebrows, and stand tall. Now try to feel depressed. It's impossible! The behavior is not congruent with feeling depressed. By visualizing and implementing a behavioral change, people can often begin to achieve their desired outcome. What is something you believe you are unable to do? How would you stand, or sit if you knew you could do it? How would you dress? Imagine it. How would your look? How would you walk?

When I teach public speaking, it's clear my students fear having to give their first speech. They breathe faster and shallower indicating a nervous state, and sometimes their skin flushes. Their hands twitch, their words stick because their mouths become dry, and their voice's quiver. Changing behaviors alone, can often change the outcomes. I ask the students to imagine themselves as successful speakers, to imagine standing tall and making eye contact, moving around before their audience, making natural gestures and using voice inflection. Once they can visualize themselves looking comfortable, their thoughts automatically change to "I can do this" and they actually become more comfortable. Not only that, they also appear more competent as speakers to their audiences. If a student reverts to feeling nervous, it clearly shows in their behaviors. To help instantly relieve them of the fear, I simply have them change their behaviors.

Most people need to visualize both the thought and behavioral change. I interviewed overweight subjects to determine their intrapersonal patterns, specifically how they spoke to themselves regarding their weight problems, and I observed the behaviors they used. Eighty percent of the subjects had negative thought patterns: "I can't lose weight, I've always been overweight, weight is a struggle, my family sabotages my efforts to lose weight, I'll be promiscuous if I lose weight, I'll die if I don't eat," to mention a few. Additionally, approximately 60% of the interviewees spoke but did not look at me while speaking. They clasped their hands, crossed their arms in a closed position, drop set their shoulders. The interviewees did this unconsciously -- they were not even aware of the behaviors they were projecting. Then I asked the interviewees to visualize both thought and behavioral changes. They imagined themselves as movie stars with perfect bodies. They imagined going through one day in a movie star's life. What time did the movie star awaken, what did they have for breakfast, lunch, dinner, snacks, to quench thirst? What exercise program did they use and how often did they exercise? Each day when the interviewees awakened they were asked to imagine themselves acting and living like a movie star. How would they hold their bodies, what would they think? They were to repeat this visualization exercise when they retired for the evening, and to listen daily to a weight loss tape to create a detailed positive mental picture of themselves preparing for their day. If they imagined eating the wrong foods, they were to change the image and imagine eating the correct foods. At the end of each day, they imaged they were successful in their endeavor. They then imagined themselves two or three months into the future at their desired weight. Seven out of ten persons lost, and maintained their weight loss, for a six-month period.

What are the characteristics you want to develop? Write them down and be specific. Now close your eyes and mentally picture yourself achieving your goal. When your thoughts and behaviors are congruent your potential is endless.

Basically, visualization offers a chance to imagine using thoughts and behaviors that are congruent and that will produce your desired goal. Congruency is a major force to acquiring the success mindset. When your thoughts and your behaviors match, your brain, both the conscious and subconscious, feels no discrepancy in what you want. If your words and your behaviors do not match, not only will you be confused, but other people will be confused too. To instill confidence, you must learn to be congruent.

What do you want? Do you want to lose weight? Stop smoking? Start exercising? Get respect? Increased confidence? Open a business? Visualization can aid in achieving whatever you desire. You can actually run your own brain and create states that support living the quality of life that you desire. Sound easy? It is! Sound too good to be true? It isn't! You still have to learn and practice the technique.

How Does Visualization Work?

By now you understand what visualization is. And from the examples and research I've discussed you probably also are beginning to understand how it works. Before we go on, let me explain how it will work for you:

Visualization is directed to the subconscious mind, which is less resistant and less critical than the conscious mind. While the conscious mind rationalizes maintaining old habits and resists new behaviors, the subconscious mind is receptive and accepting of new ideas. Your subconscious mind doesn't know the difference between your real and imagined experiences. So every time you imagine yourself successfully achieving your desired goal, you build confidence in the subconscious as if you had actually accomplished the goal.

When the subconscious believes you can accomplish a goal, it filters into the conscious state where it will be performed under the influence of the new belief system. If you can imagine actually having what you desire, you too can produce responses in the brain that help you achieve it in reality.

Visualization can help you attain goals you thought were beyond your reach. It will happen. It will happen because you are learning to utilize a part of your brain never used before, the subconscious.

You are about to learn to change your thinking and behaviors to create actions that achieve success. After all, if you continue using the same thoughts and behaviors, you will continue to get the same results. Even if you don't feel comfortable with using visualization at first, you will still benefit from learning and practicing the techniques suggested in this book.

Before we begin, I'd like you to sign a contract with yourself. Do not eliminate this step. Once it is signed, make a copy and place it a visible location.

The Contract

I, (your name:)

will not give up on myself. I will work through each chapter of this book until I have visualized clearly the thoughts and behaviors necessary to successfully achieve my goals. I will develop a daily plan, and I will follow it.

Chapter Conclusion

Picture yourself as you are right now, in a relaxed position, reading this book. Each visualization exercise begins with a relaxation exercise. If you are listening to a visualization tape or practicing self-visualization, begin by finding a comfortable position and allowing your body to relax. An effective way to relax is to begin by relaxing specific body parts: relax the muscles of your feet, then slowly work up your body, allow the ankles to relax, the calf muscles, etc. Once you are relaxed, imagine you will achieve what you desire from this book and that it feels good. Imagine you will continue reading, and working on yourself until you have a clear vision of what you desire.

Visualization can only work when you clearly see your goal. This chapter's purpose was to convince you that it's good to question how you do things, and that visualization is a useful means of creating the change needed for attaining your goals. The next chapter will help you take an in-depth look at the thoughts that may hinder your success, and help you re-frame these thoughts to create desirable outcomes.

Chapter Two

Thoughts Precede Behaviors

I f I wanted to be depressed, Monica is the person I would ask for instructions. Monica is an expert at creating a state of depression, despite the fact that she is not happy living in this state of mind.

"What can I do differently?" Monica asked.

"Perhaps you need something to look forward to," I suggested. "What is something you've always wanted to do?"

"Sky diving," she said.

"Then do that!"

She became pensive, "The parachute probably won't open. I'd splat onto the ground and die."

"At least you won't be depressed anymore."

Monica is so concerned about what might happen that she does nothing.

Thoughts, both conscious and subconscious, precede behaviors. This chapter is designed to help you discover how you think, and to re-frame the thoughts that hinder your achievement of triumphant results. As you go through this chapter, put a mark by the areas that you would like to work on.

We're going to begin by developing your conscious thoughts. In order to get what you want in your life, you first have to consciously decide it is possible.

Conscious Thought One:
Learn To Be More Flexible

In order to create a mindset for success, we need to become more mentally flexible. Try the following exercise to help you determine your mental flexibility.

Place three similar wineglasses on a table. Stand one glass on its stem, place another on the rim, lay another on its side. Now pick one of the following statements:

1) *The glasses are the same.*
2) *The glasses are the same with some differences.*
3) *The glasses are different with some similarities.*
4) *The glasses are all different.*

If you answered number (1) saying all the glasses are the same, you will generally be someone who stays on a job for 15 years or more. Although you may dislike your job, you appear to dislike change even more. You probably purchase the same food brands, shop at the same stores. If this sounds like you, you are someone who will have the most difficult time with change. You represent 5 - 10 percent of the population.

If you answered number (2) saying the glasses are the same with some differences, you like change about every seven to 10 years. You may buy a new home every seven to 10 years, change jobs, or purchase a new car. The largest percentage of the population, 55 - 60 percent, falls into this category.

If you answered number (3) saying the glasses are different with some similarities, you have no problem going after something new and different. You like change and probably go after it every 18 months to three years. Change is what keeps life interesting to you. You represent approximately 20 - 25 percent of the population.

If you answered number (4) saying the glasses are all different, you thrive on change. Even if you're happy, you seek change about every 18 months. You may also be someone who has trouble following through on a goal because before you can finish a project, you're bored with it. You represent 5 - 10 percent of the population.

Humans do not do things randomly. Our thoughts precede our behaviors, whether we are aware of these thoughts or not. Only when you become conscious of your thoughts and behaviors can you begin to make positive changes.

Perhaps you're like Kevin. Kevin's job depends on good analytical skills, but when he takes those same skills into his personal life, it often creates dissatisfaction. Kevin is single and uses his analytical skills to determine if he should continue dating each new lady that he meets.

"I shouldn't even be dating Kathy," he said. "I already know how it's going to end."

"You just met her yesterday," I said.

"Yeah, but all women want to be married. And I already know what marriage is like. Women want to take over your checkbook, you can't see your buddies anymore, there are arguments over sex, money, religion, and kids, and then of course there's the divorce and custody battle . . ."

This poor woman has not even agreed to a second date, and Kevin has futurized being married, having kids, and getting divorced. If Kevin continues this negative thought process, it will probably keep him single.

When Kevin was made aware of his thought patterns, he decided it was time to change. He made one change that has affected his life: he eliminated negative thoughts about the relationships that he considered, and today he is happily involved with a woman he believes he has a future with.

If you keep using the same negative thoughts, you'll keep getting the same negative results.

Most of us have no idea how we normally think. Most overweight people have no idea of the thoughts that precede an eating binge, let alone how many calories they consume in one day. Students want better grades, but they tell themselves that they are too tired to study, or that no matter how much they study it won't help. We want better relationships with spouses, children and co-workers, but we think there is nothing we can do to make changes. What are you thinking about right now that isn't working in your life? Where could you become more mentally flexible?

1)
2)
3)
4)
5)

Sometimes in order to get what you want in your life, you have to learn to "not" be you!

Conscious Thought Two:
Create Positive Thoughts and Attitudes

Now that you know where you want to be more mentally flexible, it's time to re-frame the negative thoughts and attitudes into positive ones. Before continuing take this simple test: begin by taking an item of jewelry and describing it with five adjectives, or sentences:

1)
2)
3)
4)
5)

Kevin looked at his watch and said: 1) it's really not very attractive; 2) it's gold, 3) it keeps time okay, 4) it's old; 5) it needs a new watchband.

Kathy looked at her watch and said: 1) it's silver so I can wear it with other silver jewelry; 2) it has a stretchy band so it's easy to get on and off; 3) it feels comfortable; 4) it keeps great time; 5) the large numbers make it easy to see.

Are your adjectives more negative, like Kevin's, or more positive, like Kathy's? These adjectives give you some idea of how you control your own thought process. Someone else could look at the same piece of jewelry and describe it more positively or more negatively. An option for changing and achieving what you desire in life is to change how you think. One way to change how you think is to change the words you use to describe situations. Those of you who are not happy with how you described the jewelry might want to begin by looking at how you describe other aspects of your life too. For example, describe yourself with five adjectives. Start by saying, "I am . . . "

1) I am ...
2) I am ...
3) I am ...
4) I am ...
5) I am ...

Perhaps you can see that your reality is a result of your own thoughts. You chose the words and thoughts to describe situations in your life. This philosophy became clearer to me when I moved to Atlanta. Moving was exciting, even though I didn't have a job. Everything I saw was new and I felt like I was on an extended vacation. Very few negative thoughts entered my mind. Even my first job telemarketing every night for three hours seemed fun and different. Life was an adventure. Within a month of my move to Atlanta, an acquaintance from

Michigan decided to move to Atlanta. I offered to let Bobbie stay in my apartment until she found her own place. Bobbie and I had similar circumstances: we had both moved to Atlanta without jobs, neither one of us knew anybody in town, and both of us had grown children we had left behind in Michigan. However, how we felt about the move to Atlanta was quite different. While I was elated, Bobbie cried herself to sleep each night. She felt terrible about leaving her son, she was disgusted because the only job she could find was working as a sales clerk in a department store, she found an apartment but hated the location, and it was clear she wasn't too pleased with me either. I refused to share her misery, which apparently annoyed her. We had the same circumstances, yet had very different reactions.

If you're not in control of your thoughts and reactions, who is? You have the power to decide if you will be angry, upset, happy, or whatever! You may not always be able to control your circumstances, but you can control your response to those circumstances.

You begin by taking control of your thoughts. Drop the negative adjectives. A snowy day is not a lousy day. It's simply a snowy day! Try to discover what is wonderful in a snowy day. Perhaps a snowy day can allow you time to do indoor activities that you might otherwise put off.

My son, Brian, believes communicating positively to himself keeps him from getting sick. Brian lived and worked with four roommates in college. Each year when a flu season arrived, his roommates became concerned that they would get the flu again, and they got it! Brian, on the other hand, firmly believed he would not get the flu or even a cold, and he has had neither for the past four years.

I am still intrigued by a woman I met on an airplane several years ago. Two days before we met, she had been in an airplane that experienced extreme turbulence. She explained it like this, "The plane dropped so fast that coffee cups were left hanging in the air, people were tumbling around like toy dolls, and most people understandably felt panicked. For some reason, I was intrigued by the experience. Since I couldn't do anything about it, I decided to consider the experience as something unique happening in my life." While most of us would not have a positive mind set under this circumstance, perhaps you can see that we do have a choice about how we react to each experience. Life doesn't have to be a drudge. It starts with your thoughts -- which you can control. And certainly your thoughts contribute to your attitude.

Charles Swindoll wrote:

*...**"I am convinced that life is 10% what happens to me and 90 % how I react to it. And so it is with you - we are in charge of our attitudes."***

Have you ever been around someone who sees everything with a negative attitude? Not for long, I bet! A sure way to isolate yourself is to continuously let others know how miserable you are. I know people who never have a good day; and most of us learn quickly to stay away from them. What amazes me is that these people don't seem to understand why they have become isolated.

Evelyn is a perfect example of someone with a negative attitude. I met Evelyn at a dance. She is a terrific dancer; she can do any dance, yet she is rarely asked to dance. At first I thought the men were intimidated because she was such a good dancer, yet I watched men dance with many other women who were also terrific dancers and often less attractive than Evelyn. My curiosity led me to approach Evelyn and comment how much I enjoyed watching her dance.

"I'm better when I'm with a male who can lead," she scoffed. "I don't know why I bother coming to this dance club. I don't like it here. Last week this club met with another group in South Carolina, and I thought that maybe they'd have some good dancers. Wrong! I drove 300 miles, by myself, to get to the dance because nobody had room for even one extra person in their car. Then I couldn't find anyone to share a hotel room with. And after all that driving, there were still no-good dancers. I had a miserable time."

"Wow!" Not a surprise that no one had room for Evelyn in their car, and no one wanted to share a room with her. It is difficult to be around people who are never happy.

Reality is What We Individually Create

What is interesting about negative people is why they have such poor attitudes. Evelyn had always wanted to be a dance instructor, but had given up her dream when she married. Her husband did not want her to work. "Are you still married?" I asked. "No, she said, "and I had no work skills to care for myself after the divorce. To pay my bills I started working as a secretary, I've been a secretary for ten years. I can retire in another ten years, if I can hold out that long," she rolled her eyes.

People with a poor attitude often feel stuck in a way of life they dislike. They may attribute this to several causes: perhaps they gave up a dream when they married, or decided to stay at home with their children, 2) perhaps they gave up on a dream because they, or someone else, believed they could never achieve it, 3) perhaps they felt it was too late to go after what they wanted because they had too much time invested with a company, 4) perhaps they don't want to lose a pension, 5) perhaps they've grown accustomed to a lifestyle or income, 6) perhaps they fear starting a new job because they'd have to give up vacation time, 7) perhaps they have tried going after a dream and failed, 8) perhaps they think they are too old to follow dreams, 9) or any number of reasons that keep us from happiness.

Consider this:

Is the payoff sufficient for doing what you don't want to do with the rest of your life?

Your answer to this question may be "yes," but if the answer is "no," go back to your "comfort zone" list on page 16. Put a check by the items you are not happy with, and that you want to change. Put a star by the items you would like to try, but have yet to, and brainstorm a list of reasons for trying these items.

Brainstorm Ideas

Brainstorming is an important step for achieving mental flexibility and turning thoughts into positive behaviors. Do not omit it. Brainstorming was developed by advertising executive Alex Osborn and is a popular method for finding creative ideas and thoughts. There are several rules you will want to follow when you brainstorm: 1) Do not criticize your ideas as you list them. Many people think of an idea, and reject it before they can even write it down. In this stage simply write down every thought that comes into your head for ten minutes. Do this for each item you've checked on your comfort zone list. 2) Think of several absolutely wild, way-out solutions too. The more ridiculous the better. This helps stimulate creativity. 3) Come up with as many ideas as you can. The greater number of ideas, the more likelihood of finding a winner. 4) Combine and improve ideas as you go. In other words, let new ideas build on previous ideas.

Once you've generated ideas through the brainstorming exercise, you can evaluate, analyze, research and talk to others before making a final decision. Take the time to consider each idea: 1) Does it meet the criteria you are after? 2) What are its consequences? 3) Are there alternatives? 4) Is the decision based on facts, assumptions, and inferences that are reasonable, accurate and valid? 5) Challenge the validity of each option.

One of the items on my list that I was not happy with was living in cold weather. Here's how my list looked:

Not happy with:	Options list:
Cold weather	Change thoughts about cold weather
	Try winter sports
	Isolate myself until winter is over
	Wear warmer clothes
	Move

The next step is to consider all aspects of each option. For the option of *"moving"* mine looked like this:

Moving from family/friends	Fly home/drive
	Make new friends
	Move to East Coast so I can drive home

Sometimes having a negative thought on a subject, especially if you are normally a positive person, is enough to let you know something needs revision. No matter how hard I tried, I found it difficult to communicate positively about living in a cold climate. Since I didn't want to harbor negative thoughts about where I was living the remainder of my life, the choice was to move to a warmer climate. But I also knew that moving would create something else I would not be happy with, being away from family and friends. Again, I had to list options for becoming happier. If I stayed on the East Coast, I could fly home within two hours, or drive home in ten hours. With time, I would make new friends. And family and friends could visit me. Moving met my criteria.

Our goals often change with time. What made you happy ten years ago may be making you miserable today. Ten years ago I didn't mind cold weather, I enjoyed playing winter sports with my sons. Today, I find cold weather intolerable. If you have ten, twenty or thirty years remaining, why not choose what makes you happy? Going after what makes you happy is a strong variable for creating a positive change in your attitude. Janis is a testimony to this.

Conscious Thought Three: Go After What Makes You Happy

Janis married a second time after living single for nine years. Unfortunately she was miserable within nine months of getting married. She had married an alcoholic who had no plans to begin recovery. Six years later, Janis is still married and still miserable. When I asked Janis what concerned her about leaving the marriage, she said she didn't want to start over again. In lieu of starting over, Janis has started smoking again, has gained 50 pounds, and she is so negative about life that she has developed an attitude that has pushed family and friends away. Admittedly she was miserable in her marriage, and probably with her life. Recently, Janis decided her happiness and sanity were more important to her. She is now divorced, and has lost 50 pounds. She is still smoking, but feeling good about herself and her life. She is dating again and hopes to find a fulfilling relationship. She had no hope of a fulfilling relationship if she had stayed where she was.

Think about this for a moment: if you could do anything you wanted, what would that be? Before you continue, look at your comfort zone list again. In a hierarchical order, list the five goals you most want to achieve:

1.
2.
3.
4.
5.

Once you have these items listed, write the immediate afterthought you have for each item. Dan's first wish was to be a musician. He wanted to cut albums and tour the country in a band. He barely finished this sentence when he added "but I can't make a living as a musician. The average musician probably makes $10,000.00 a year."

To some people, $10,000.00 might be enough, so what was stopping Dan? "I have a home mortgage," he said, "two car payments, a wife who wouldn't want me touring, and a baby on the way." Dan is 28 years old; he is a highly creative person working as a computer technician but he wants to be a musician. If Dan continues in the corporate environment until he's 65, he'll have 37 more years to convince himself he shouldn't go after the one thing he really wants in his life, to be a musician. Dan has the attitude that being a musician means he must immediately change his lifestyle and tour the world. If he brainstormed, Dan might find there are many more options available for him, for instance: he could work part-time and join a band

and play locally, or continue his full time job and play in a band on weekends.

Being happy doesn't always come naturally. It takes effort, and it's a challenge to get rid of the thoughts and attitudes that defeat your happiness and dreams. Take a moment right now to brainstorm the options you have for creating your own reality and achieving your dreams! Be creative! Don't forget to add the items from the "mental flexibility" list on page 35.

Conscious Thought Four: Believe in Yourself

How many times have you heard people say "I can't . . . I can't dance; I can't do math; I can't go to college; I can't take tests." They say "I can't ... whatever, and they really can't! It's nearly impossible to get the things you want, or to accomplish the things you want if you constantly tell yourself "I can't."

Think back to what it was like to be a kid. Remember the first time you tried to ride a bike, or roller skate, or jump rope? Did you master these skills the first time out? Probably not. But did you give up? Probably not. There was a determination, a conviction that you not only had to do it, but you would. You tried everyday, over and over, day after day, until you did finally mastered it. You never thought of giving up, you believed you could do it, and it was just a matter of time before you achieved it. I remember spending an entire summer, two months, learning to ride my bike with no hands. It didn't matter to me how long it took, I just knew I had to do it!

To get what you want, you first have to believe you can achieve it. Thoughts precede behaviors. This is not to say you should never consider the problems that may get in the way of achieving a desired outcome. You need to access problem areas so you know how to deal with them if they should come up. For instance, if you discover you are biologically unable to have children, believing in yourself may make you feel better for a while, but it probably won't help you have a child. You may have to adjust this dream in order to achieve it. You may need to consider other alternatives; otherwise you really are stuck.

Whenever I feel stuck, I think of my friend John. In 1997 John was diagnosed with cancer, and in my opinion, he had every reason to feel stuck. He had no health insurance, no family living close, and no chance for a future; he had been given 2-5 years to live, yet John had a positive attitude about life. John lived for the good in each day.

John firmly believed that worrying about his condition was more devastating than the cancer. "I used to worry if I'd make it through the night, only to find myself here the next morning; I worried about losing time from work, only to discover that work is a gratifying distraction; I worried about how my family and friends would react, only to find a sense of support and comfort from them. I finally decided that life was literally too short for me to waste it worrying. I just decided to stop worrying and to enjoy the time I had left."

"What will you do?" I asked.

"Everything I've been putting off because I

thought I could do it tomorrow. In a strange sense this cancer has made me begin my life."

"Today" is all John has. Today, this moment, is all any of us knows we have for sure! It's time to make the most of it. Having the option to even consider a future is really exciting. It means you're not dying, but it doesn't necessarily mean you're living. Think for a moment, how do you know when someone is really living? Whenever I think about someone who is really alive, and believes in herself, I think of Mary. She enjoys life, and part of her enjoyment is that she continues to learn and grow. She takes classes, she tries different things to help her discover what she enjoys, and when she finds something she likes, she puts her heart into it. Mary took writing classes and started writing advertisements in her spare time. She didn't give up on writing when she received rejection slips, nor did she doubt her writing ability because she wasn't published. She just kept learning and growing and submitting her work, and occasionally she made a sale. Mary would love to write full-time, but she doesn't make enough money to support herself as a writer, yet. But she believes in her ability to write. She believes her dream can fit into her lifestyle, despite the fact that she has five children, two car payments, a boat payment, and friends and family who think she should grow up and quit her foolishness.

People who achieve what they desire in life believe in themselves and in finding their own happiness. They simply don't give up on themselves or their dreams easily. My son wants to be a rock star. If someone else can make it as a rock star, why not my son? Why not you if this is your dream?

I still have family members trying to convince me that if I were a good parent, I would convince my son to give up his dream of becoming a rock star and to get a real job. How sad that we feel our job as parents is to restrict our children's dreams, to make them follow the road we feel is acceptable instead of helping them discover what they feel is acceptable. It is even sadder that any one of us allows another to control our lives.

If any parents had reason to try and restrict their child it would have been Sandy's parents. By age eleven Sandy was nearly blind. She had big dreams despite the impending affliction. Although her parents were concerned about her getting along in life, they never restricted her dreams. Today, Sandy is single, she owns a home in Detroit, has a vacation cottage in Upper Michigan, and she runs a successful computer sales business.

I commented once that she did not seem to let anything hold her back. "My biggest obstacle is not my blindness, it's other people who believe I have a disability. I have an inconvenience," she said.

Although Sandy qualifies for social security, she prefers to work. Additionally, she has no help from family because her parents and her brother moved to Arizona ten years ago.

Sandy expects to succeed in life. Despite her blindness, she has set no boundaries for herself. She snow skis, water-skis, travels, and enjoys life! How does a blind person snow ski? With a guide talking her down the hill.

I asked Sandy if she was ever afraid. "Sure," she said, "aren't you sometimes afraid?"

"Yes, but I'm not blind."

"It's the mind's eye that matters," she said. "Belief in ourselves is the natural response; we learn to be skeptical."

So how do we strengthen a belief in ourselves and eliminate this skepticism? After all, we have been programmed by the people who care for us to be skeptical. We have been taught to stop thinking for ourselves and to conform to what our parents and teachers deem acceptable. Consequently, we stop believing in our own feelings and desires. We forget how to think for ourselves. In fact, by the time we reach college age, we have learned to stop believing in our instincts quite well.

Stanley Milgram (1956, 1963, 1964,) an experimenter at Yale, designed a series of experiments to determine whether individuals who received a command from an authority figure would obey, even though the authority figure had no real power to compel obedience. In the experiment, students were ordered to give a lab worker an electric shock whenever he got a word wrong. The more wrong words, the greater the shock. The lab worker, although never actually shocked, was trained to writhe in pain and to pound on the wall as though the shock was intensifying. Despite the apparent pain, the intensity of the shock was to increase with wrong answers.

Although it was predicted the students would refuse to administer extremely strong shocks to innocent victims, most students obeyed the command and continued shocking the victim up to the maximum level. Only 13 percent of the students defied the experimenter and stopped. Even when the intensity of the shock reached the danger level and beyond, well over half of the students were still administering shocks to the victims.

Many of these students admitted they felt what they were doing was wrong. So why didn't they believe in their own instincts? Why don't you believe in your own instincts? It's time to take control and go for what you want out of life!

I saw Dustin Hoffman in a television interview saying that being an actor was all he could imagine for himself yet he never expected to be a successful actor. He was just doing what he loved. He knew there were no guarantees that he would make it. Nancy Kerrigan on a Regis and Kathie Lee show in December 1997 said she never thought about being an Olympic winner. Kerrigan said she skated because she enjoyed it and she wanted to do the best she could each time she was on the ice.

Where we would be if Thomas Edison had stopped believing that he could produce the electric light? Or if Henry Ford, or a number of others had stopped before achieving their dreams? You can bet there were a number of people trying to convince these folks to give up. It is truly a good thing some people believe in their ability and dreams. These confident few move the whole world forward.

While I was working on a Ph.D., I met a number of students who decided to quit the doctoral program. It's the longest of the degree programs to complete, and it's the most expensive. Many wanted a guarantee that the Ph.D. would increase their chances for success, or enhance their pay, and when they received no guarantee, they quit. The people who did complete the Ph.D. had some common characteristics. They believed in themselves, they believed that they were capable of achieving their dream and they were willing do to whatever it took to complete the program. Many students I spoke with had family and friends who tried to convince them to drop the dream of a Ph.D. and get on with their lives. Many of my own family members believed a Ph.D. would hinder my job prospects. To succeed, we must control our own thoughts.

Conscious Thought Five: Take Control of Your Thoughts

Believing in yourself means taking control of your thoughts. One way to take control of your thoughts is to use re-framing techniques. Every time you have a thought that inhibits you from achieving what you desire in life, write that thought down. Next, find two alternatives, two productive thoughts to take its place. It's time for you to start running your own brain instead of allowing it to run on automatic pilot.

Amy's inhibiting thoughts were regarding weight loss. She repeated the following paragraph, word for word, every time she discussed her weight. "I can't lose weight. My doctor wants me to lose weight but I can't. I don't even eat that much. I guess I'll just have to accept myself as I am."

Following is the alternative, productive thought that Amy repeats now. "I can lose weight. My doctor wants me to lose weight and I will do it for my health and well being. I will eat healthy and watch my calories and fat intake. I can lose weight if I continue this thought process."

Once you have a productive thought written

down, begin the following exercise.

Exercise

Take a comfortable position. Focus on relaxing the muscles from your feet all the way to the top of your head. This process may take five to ten minutes. Once you are relaxed, begin reciting your productive thoughts. If an inhibiting thought comes to mind during the exercise, or anytime, immediately think of your productive thought. Imagine how easy it will be to replace negative thoughts with productive thoughts and to produce the outcomes you desire.

Take notice of the time of day you have inhibiting thoughts? Is it early in the day or late? Do you have inhibiting thoughts at home or away from home? Are you alone or with someone else? Imagine what it will feel like to control your thoughts no matter what the circumstance, and no matter what someone else says or does? Take one day at a time, one hour at a time, and allow yourself to experience success at controlling your thoughts.

Be Patient

Part of believing in yourself is learning to be patient with yourself. It may easily take 21 days of practice before you gain control over your thoughts. I suggest you practice daily for the first month, then once a week for maintenance. The more you practice, the faster you will gain control of your thoughts, and the quicker you will see the actions and goals you desire becoming a reality.

The future is what you decide to make it.

The purpose of this chapter was to help you discover that thoughts precede behaviors. The next chapter develops the behaviors necessary to create your desired results.

Chapter Three

Preparing Your Action Plan

ill Rogers said, "Even if you're on the right track, you'll get run over if you just sit there." Correct thoughts create the foundation for the correct behaviors, but you have to determine which behaviors to adjust in order to attain your goals. Successful people know what they want out of life, and they go after it. This chapter looks at the behaviors you will need to achieve your goals.

Attaining your goals is not about luck like many people prefer to think, it is about being prepared when good luck comes your way. When I decided to teach continuing education, I prepared a number of classes and sent out samples hoping colleges would want my services. It was a year before a college in Georgia called and asked if I could fill in for a customer service instructor who had become ill. I was asked to teach a six-hour seminar. I agreed, feeling that luck was on my side. "Good," the voice on the other end of the phone said, "then we'll see you tomorrow morning at 8:00 a.m."

Tomorrow morning! I had expected the voice on the other end of the phone to say "See you next month." Fortunately, I had a customer service seminar prepared; otherwise I would have had to turn this assignment down. The moral of this story:

When luck comes your way be ready to open that door and welcome it in!

Take a look at your comfort zone list again (page 16). If you have yet to prioritize these items, do it now. What is the number one item on your list? Now let's figure out what behaviors you must correct to achieve it.

Behavior One: Try something different!

We all know the old adage, "If at first you don't succeed, _try, try again._" I'd like you to consider an alternative: "If at first you don't succeed, try something different." Almost anything different is probably better than continuing to do something that is getting poor results.

I worked with a woman who was trying to play a VCR tape by pressing the play button on the remote unit. Normally this would work, but after five tries, it was clear something else needed to be considered. "No, this should do it," she insisted, hitting the play button again with no success.

Finally, feeling completely frustrated, she gave up pushing the buttons and called maintenance. Maintenance switched channels and the VCR tape worked. My colleague felt very foolish. Why hadn't she thought of that herself? Why hadn't she listened to colleagues who told her to "try something else"?

Why do we persist in the same old solutions, over and over, when all the evidence points to failure? The fact is that most of us don't like change. We are simply more comfortable doing things the way we always have, even if what we're doing doesn't work. Even when another way is proven more effective, we fight change. Do you remember your initial reaction when computers first became available? I know people who quit their jobs because they were required to learn to use a computer. Today, I know people who would quit their job if computers were not available to them!

Not only do we fight change in ourselves, we also resist change in others. When Mick and Don decided to open a hair salon doing haircuts and blow dry work only, friends and family did all they could to deter them. The excitement Mick and Don felt about telling others of their plan to open a business quickly vanished. Rather than wishing them well, friends felt compelled to share their negative thoughts. One friend told them they would be out of business in six months because a hair salon could not survive with customers returning only every six weeks for a haircut. Another friend pointed out that 80% of new businesses fail within the first three years.

Another friend reported having taken a second mortgage on his house, only to lose everything when his business failed within ten months of the grand opening.

Family members are especially relentless in their efforts to keep things just the way they are. Although families are concerned for our welfare, they are just as concerned with changes that might upset the life they have worked so hard to create, and you may be part of that life. At age 26, I realized that my life was exactly what my family had decided was appropriate. I was married, I worked part-time while raising two children, and my parents lived close so they could visit often and baby-sit, which everyone enjoyed. Family members tried to discourage my sister Pat and me from opening a business. We heard one horror story after another about relatives who attempted to go into a business; each story ended in failure and bad feelings. Pat and I had to decide if we were on earth to keep the family happy, or if we wanted to fulfill personal goals. We chose to pursue personal goals: we opened our business, and we were fortunate to maintain it for ten years. Pat and I are still the best of friends, too.

Defying friends and family was one of the most difficult aspects of following our dream. Research indicates that such independence of mind is difficult for all of us. A study on conformity theory indicates our desire to "go along" often leads us to give up on what we believe. In one university study nine people were asked to look at four lines drawn on a board before them. Three of the four lines were the same length. The fourth line was obviously shorter.

Each person was told to simply state that the lines were the same lengths when asked. Now a tenth person was brought into the room. The first nine people were asked one at a time if the lines were the same, or different lengths. One by one all nine people said the lines were the same lengths. It was apparent that the tenth person did not agree. Sometimes the tenth person nudged the person next to him or her or snickered or looked puzzled, as if to say "do you believe this?" But in a significant number of rounds when it was time for the tenth person to indicate if the lines were the same length or different, this person went along with the group by stating "the lines are the same."

Like it or not, we all have a tendency to follow the crowd. I was recently with a friend who drove up to the longest line at a toll road booth while another booth had no cars. "Why don't you go to the other booth?" I asked. I was rather sarcastically told, "Don't you think if that booth were open the other cars would already be there?" Several other cars filed in behind us, until one car finally went to the second booth and quickly passed through. In unfamiliar situations, we seem to believe that other people must know better, so we tend to follow them.

Understanding our tendency to conform and follow the crowd helps us become more independent. When my sister, Pat, and I realized our tendency to compromise our beliefs when confronted with group pressure, we made several changes that helped us with our decision to open a business. We tried something different. How did we overcome the tendency to conform? Here are some options to keep you on track:

First, simply stay away from people with negative comments. If Pat and I found ourselves in the company of someone offering negative comments about our decision to open our business, we asked them to change the subject. If changing the subject was too difficult, we removed ourselves from the situation. Sometimes it is simply best to stay away from people or places that are not supportive. Try something different! Pat and I both decided that mental well being was imperative at this critical first stage of our new business. So we avoided certain people until it was comfortable again.

Second, manage your concerns instead of hiding from them. Pat and I decided to keep a list of our concerns, and once a week, for one hour, we allowed ourselves to delve into them. We resolved the concerns that we could, and we saved the others for a future date. An interesting thing happened! Most of the concerns on our list never became a reality, so we never had to deal with them. We didn't let our concerns stop us from going after our dream, and we didn't let them become a source of hidden anxiety either.

It's difficult to understand that family and friends who love us can also destroy our zest for life if we allow their fears and concerns to rule our existence. I have enough fears and concerns of my own, thank you; I don't need to take theirs on too.

Third, consider the ulterior motives of people offering negativity. People do not always mean well in their attempts to help us consider the effects of change. When I decided to move to Georgia, my closet friend, Marsha, started watching the weather channel and reported to me daily how hot the summers are in Atlanta. When I mentioned that I wanted a warmer climate, and she realized her report would not deter my moving, she told me stories about people who had moved away from family and were miserable trying to make it on their own. "Females need to be near family and friends," she advised. "People take advantage of single females. I know someone who nearly went bankrupt after a move. The moving company stole her furniture, the apartment she planned to move into wasn't ready and she ended up in a motel for a month, the motel-cleaning people took her credit cards . . ."

"Wow! Do you see anything positive about my move?" I asked.

"No. I'm going to miss you. I wish I could say I hope everything goes great for you, but I don't feel that way. If you go, there is a part of me that hopes you will fail because I want you to come back."

My best friend was hoping I would fail! When friends and family offer warnings and negative reports, they may really be worried about how change will affect their lives.

Fourth, create confidence. Another way to help family and friends cope with your desire to go after what makes you happy is to demonstrate confidence in your decision. We admire confidence, even if we don't always agree with it. How would you talk if you were confident about obtaining your goals? For example, how would you talk about losing weight if you were confident you could do it? To create confidence regarding my move to Atlanta, I said, "I have lived in Detroit as a single female for years. I'm used to taking care of myself, and I take precautions to keep myself safe in big cities. I have no doubt I'll get along fine in Atlanta; I've gotten along fine in Detroit."

Unfortunately, words alone do not create much impact, or build confidence. Research shows that only 7% of a message's impact is conveyed in words. Words are cheap, and people often say things they don't mean. So how do we add to the confidence of our message? One way is tone of voice.

Tone of voice -- the intensity of our voice, how loud or soft we speak, and how fast we speak, adds 38% of the impact to our message. We need to sound confident; we need to sound as if we mean what we say. However, research also indicates that what people actually do has more impact than what they say, or how they say it.

Non-verbal behaviors, or body language, provide 55% of the impact of a message. Often we are not aware of the messages we are sending non-verbally. Muggers watch the body language of a prospective victim before they attack. The way someone walks down the street lets the mugger know if this person will put up a fight, or retreat. What does your body language tell your friends and family? Will you put up a fight or retreat? People simply will not bother you if you appear confident. When you appear confident, people believe you will do what you say, they believe in the product you are selling, they accept the idea you are suggesting, they become convinced you are capable of handling yourself in any situation.

For the next week, be aware of the words you use, your tone of voice, and your body language. If you are not happy with the results you are getting, try something different, because if you continue doing things the same way you always have, you can expect no change. How many times have you let others stop you from living the life you desire? Why did you take your last job? If you don't work, why don't you? Why do you live in this state? Why did you buy your last car? Why do you live where you do? Why do you keep the relationships you've chosen? Why do you exercise, or not exercise? Why don't you have a hobby? Why do you eat the foods you do? Why do you get mad at your spouse, children, or friends? Are you fulfilling personal goals, or are you trying to accommodate the desires of family and friends? List everything you have ever complained about too. What rules govern your life? Which rules did you impose upon yourself? Which rules have others imposed upon you? This is your chance to eliminate the rules you don't agree with, revise others, or come up with rules that make sense to you. Consider the rules you have imposed upon others, too. Are you holding family or friends back from achieving their own goals? It would be wonderful if your goals made everybody happy, but in reality, there is only one person you can know for sure has been made happy, or unhappy by your decisions. That is you.

In theory it always sounds good to say, "try something different," but in reality it's not always so easy to achieve. Most of us have financial obligations, and family and friends who are not supportive, and often in order to achieve one goal, we have to give up on something else we enjoy. I wanted to move to a warmer climate, so I had to give up closeness to family. You may want to lose ten pounds, but you'll have to give up ice cream. If you want a college degree, you have to give up time and money. We each have to decide:

Is the payoff sufficient for doing what we don't want to do with the rest of our lives?

What can you do differently?

Behavior Two: Setting Your Goals

To assist you in setting new goals, we're going to look at communication theories. Please answer the following questions pertaining to your goals:

1) What outcome do I desire?
2) Is the goal specific enough to permit direct planning and action, or is the goal general and abstract?
3) Does the goal involve me personally; meaning is there a behavior I must change to accomplish the goal?
4) Is the goal realistic? Can it be accomplished during a specific time frame?
5) Can others help me work on this goal?
6) Is this my true goal, or is it a front for a subtle or hidden goal?
7) What barriers do I anticipate in reaching my goal?

The answers to these questions are

imperative for getting headed in the right direction. Not only do you need to be specific in what you want, you need to keep moving toward your goal and you need sufficient powers of observation to know if you are moving toward your outcome. One way to do this is by working on smaller "chunks" rather than focusing on the end result.

Take One Step At A Time

Although it's important to know the end goal you desire, in order to attain that goal you have to focus on the smaller steps needed for achieving it. Right about now you're probably saying, "Well who doesn't know that?" We all know it; the problem is we don't do it! When we stay focused on the end goal, we often get bogged down thinking it's too difficult to attain. As a result we never get started.

Think about it like this. Have you ever been to Sea World? Have you ever wondered how they get a whale to jump over a rope that is ten feet above the water level? If the trainers focus all of their attention on the main goal of getting that whale over a rope ten feet above water level, they would probably never accomplish it. However, if they focus on smaller steps, they can build up to the main goal. They start by laying a rope on the bottom of the pool and waiting for the whale to cross over it. Every time the whale goes over the rope, they offer a positive reinforcement, a fish. Then they lift the rope one-foot, still offering a fish as a reward once the whale crosses over the rope. Eventually, the rope can be lifted high enough that the whale could also go under the rope, but the whale only gets the fish when it goes over the rope. Small steps are taken until the whale is going over the rope even when it is lifted above the water level.

This same philosophy pertains to your personal goal attainment. Take small steps and reward yourself with positive self-talk, or a gift, or maybe you prefer a fish. But stop focusing only on the end goal.

Here's a human example: if Frank had taken small steps he might have his bathroom wallpapered, today. In Frank's mind, once he started the job of stripping the old wallpaper, he couldn't stop because the job would be too messy to have it drag on for days. So once he started stripping the paper, he thought he would have to keep working until the job was completed. He figured it would be a 15-hour job. Because he was focusing only on the completed job and how much work it entailed, he never started the job! Two years later, the bathroom still has the same wallpaper.

While we need to know what direction we are going, if we stay focused on the end result, it's often paralyzing! While working on my Ph.D., I met a number of people who dropped out of the program, including Jim, because he focused on the end result. Jim was focused on actually having that Ph.D. in hand. His immediate afterthought was, "It will take four to six years to complete the program because I'll have to work full-time and be a part-time student. I need 90 credits, which will take forever. Since I have to work, I'll have little time for homework, and I'm certain to have no social life." With thoughts like this, it is no wonder so few people go on for this advanced degree. In contrast, people who complete their degrees learn to take smaller steps. They map out a strategy for their entire program, detailing the classes needed to complete the Ph.D., but then they began focusing on one semester of classes at a time.

Nadine listed all the classes she needed, then focused on taking two classes each semester. "I decided as long as I enjoyed learning, I would continue taking two classes each semester. My final goal of graduating was five years off; I just had to quit thinking about how far away that was because when I did think about it, I immediately thought, I can't make it!" Nadine received her Ph.D. in 1996. At the end of each semester, her grades were an indication that she was heading in the right direction. If she received a poor grade, she knew she had to study more. She gave herself little rewards for passing each semester too. She took weekend vacations to a hotel with a pool and hot tub. She occasionally enjoyed dining out, seeing a movie, or the luxury of a massage after months of feeling tense.

Having a goal is great, but it is not enough. You have to take the small steps to accomplish it! List the steps you perceive as necessary for achieving your goal.

Behavior Three:
End Procrastination

Recently, I met a young woman who wanted to write a book. She had procrastinated about beginning this book for nearly a year, "I keep thinking about the time commitment," she said, "how will I find the time to write 300 pages?"

The answer is obvious. You write one page at a time. Writing one page is easy. So just keep writing one page. Write one page a day, or one page a week, and eventually you have a book.

When goals seem unattainable, we often react by doing nothing at all. That is, we procrastinate. If you find yourself procrastinating, take smaller steps. It sounds so simple doesn't it? Yet many of us stay focused on the completed goal and because it sounds overwhelming, we never get started. If you still find yourself procrastinating even after focusing on smaller steps, search for a new behavior, a new action. That is just what James did.

James opened a home-based consulting business. He decided in order to sell his services, he had to mail 50 letters per day, 50! This is an admirable goal. Unfortunately, the goal was also overwhelming. Each night when he came home from his full-time job, and considered mailing 50 letters between 6:00 p.m. and 9:00 p.m., he found himself distracted and unable to sit down and begin working. The goal James had set for himself was not attainable.

When I suggested James consider mailing 10 letters per night, he still procrastinated. "I won't get any sales volume on 10 letters a night," he said.

James needed another strategy. He decided to hire a high school student to do a mass mailing for him.

Ending procrastination means actually

doing what you say you are going to do. Keep adjusting the project, or your behaviors, until you can attain your goal. How many of you have tried to lose weight? Trying to lose 25 pounds is overwhelming. Even five pounds is difficult for some people. However, losing one pound is not so bad. So, lose one pound! To lose one pound you have to eliminate approximately 3,500 calories. That's a lot of calories to give up, unless you divide it by seven days . . . then it's only 500 calories per day. If 500 calories is still too much too give up, eliminate 250 calories per day. You will lose one pound every two weeks, and only have to give up one half of a candy bar a day! Make it attainable; then do what you say you're going to do.

Behavior Four:
Stop Sabotaging Your Goals

We all know people who have joined a gym, or started an exercise program, only to become frustrated and quit. I was no exception to this. I joined a karate class that started out with more than 100 people. Within three weeks there were only ten people left! By the fourth week there were nine people left, I had quit too! The karate class met three times each week and exercised students to the point of exhaustion. My body had not recovered from one night of strained muscles before I was inflicting muscle strain on it again. I expected too much of myself and ended up quitting.

I decided jogging might suit me better. I even found a friend who agreed to jog with me.

David was an avid jogger. The first morning, with lots of prodding from David, we did a combination jog and walk for six miles. It took me two hours of lying flat out on couch to recover, and another two days before the muscles in my legs allowed me to stand straight. It was almost a year before I decided to exercise again. This time I started out walking one mile per day. I built up to jogging a mile a day, then two miles. I worked at a pace my body could tolerate. I didn't let someone else decide the pace I should keep. I found my own pace, and I've been a jogger ever since.

We have a tendency to sabotage goals by expecting too much of ourselves. Once we have sabotaged our goals, we are often convinced there is no use trying anything else because we have already proven we can't make it. So, make the goal attainable. Start by taking one small step, take one class, write one page, make one phone call, eat one less candy bar, walk one mile.

What goals have you sabotaged? Or do you prefer to blame others for sabotaging your goals? In my business communication classes I ask the following question, "How many of you see yourself as a leader?" Most students raise their hands. Then I ask the students to form groups of five people. Each group has the task of picking one person as their leader. Nearly all of the groups end up with a male as their leader, even the groups that are predominantly female. My next question is "Why aren't you a leader?" The usual response is "we just picked the person who said he or she wanted it." Exactly!

When you want something, you have to ask for it! Things rarely drop into your lap. If you want a raise, you have to ask for it. If you want a promotion, you have to ask for it. Males apparently ask for what they want more often. I've had classes with five males and 20 females and the five males all end up as the leaders. The females rationalize that this is just a game. But in both games and in an actual business setting, males end up in leadership positions more often, partly because they ask for the position.

It is a nice dream to think whatever you want will fall into your lap, yet it is more likely you'll achieve success by working toward a goal and using the communication strategies taught in this book. As a reassuring note, you might consider that you don't have to do it alone. Many people have already done what you want to accomplish. Why not learn from them?

Behavior Five: Continued Learning

Many theorists believe that if we follow the strategies of successful people, we will also become more successful. This is an excellent strategy if we can figure out what successful people actually do.

Experts often cannot explain what they do. One reason people attend college is to learn from experts who are also teachers and who are capable of explaining what has worked, or has not worked. If you're not in a college degree program, there are many organized programs to help you: continuing education offers day and evening classes to help you learn just about any new skill from computers to business writing and speaking, management skills or starting your own business. Professional organizations like American Society for Training and Development offer workshops focusing on training needs. The Small Business Administration (SBA) offers help to individuals for free. SBA has professionals who have worked in the field and now volunteer their time to help others. Product lines usually have seminars to increase the motivation of their sales staff, to teach product knowledge and to offer marketing tips. Why not take advantage of this help?

The problem is we often don't even know there is a better way, and so we don't seek new knowledge? Here's the reason to seek knowledge: you have nothing to compare your present reality to. In essence you become stuck in one version of reality, your own. Life teaches us that there is no such thing as only one way to accomplish a goal. Cindy learned this lesson while selling cosmetic products.

Cindy had tried everything to get her cosmetics business off the ground: she made evening phone calls, she mailed information on the products, she offered free facials, but her business did not become successful until she used the ideas of Jena. Jena was a speaker at a monthly sales consulting meeting. And she is apparently a very successful salesperson; she pulled up in a Cadillac and had more gold on her body than Fort Knox. Despite her success, Jena continued the practice of attending monthly meetings and had one message for new consultants, "Keep attending meetings and learning from others."

Knowledge is Power - Hobbes, Leviathan

Knowledge gives you the opportunity to explore more options, to try the options out, and to find out what works best for you. On a monthly basis, Cindy continues to meet with her sales consulting group to learn new sales techniques. Her sales volume has increased and so has her motivation to help others become successful. She has her own message for new consultants now: "Groups make better decisions than individuals," a philosophy strongly supported by research.

Time and again, research has shown that groups make better decisions than individuals. One study that set out to prove this was the NASA Moon Survival problem developed by Hall and Watson. In this simulation, group members are asked to view themselves as the crew of a space flight. They were forced to crash-land on the lighted side of the moon approximately 200 miles from their designated rendezvous point with the mother ship. With the exception of 15 items presented to the group, all other items were destroyed in the crash. The task facing the group was to rank order the list by its importance to their survival. Groups made better decisions and survived more often than individuals. Why? There were more brains to work out the problem. Even in a situation where no one actually knew the correct answer, groups problem-solved more effectively.

Hirokawa (1982) found that groups reach higher quality decisions than individuals if a consensus decision is reached using a systematic strategy. A consensus means the group cannot vote on a solution to the problem, but they must keep discussing until everyone agrees.

A number of other researchers believe the group members should individually brainstorm solutions to ideas before beginning to debate about the best solution. Ideas should be listed for everyone to see and the group should be allowed to discuss and build upon each other's ideas without criticism (Dunnette, Campbell & Jassted, 1963; Bouchard, 1972,). Silence periods should be allowed so group members can think (Ruback, Dabbs & Hopper, 1984). Then the group should be asked to reach a consensus decision before the solution is implemented. If group members agree with the solution, they will be motivated to follow through on the solution, and to make their solution work, even if it is not the best of all possible solutions.

Knowledge is wonderful, yet to truly benefit from knowledge you also have to put it into practice, then you must periodically reassess what you have learned and determine what works for you.

Behavior Six:
Reassessment of Goals

Within 30 days, re-examine your goals in light of your experience. List what you have done. Be specific: What is hindering your progress? What is helping your progress? If you are not getting the outcome you desire, change something. If you are happy, don't change.

You'd be surprised how many successful

people decide to change something that is working. Experimenting is great! It may help you find a new or better way to achieve your outcome. But to experiment without monitoring the results or without an understanding of why things are working could produce a disaster. Here's an example:

A sales-based company had finally reached its financial goals. Things were working, they had a good product, a good presentation package and a staff that looked and acted professional. The sales staff, both male and female, had always worn suits when calling on organizational clients mostly because their clients also wore suits. The company president suddenly decided that wearing casual clothing was appropriate. The change in attire became immediately effective. Wearing a shirt or blouse, slacks or a skirt, with no tie or jacket was acceptable. While the sales company's original clients appeared unconcerned by this change in attire, new clients were apparently not impressed. A distinct reduction in new orders was noted at a six-month assessment. The sales staff went back to wearing suits but not before a problem was created. Many new clients had already been lost over that six-month period. My question is "why did this company wait six months to reassess?" Not only did the company lose new business; but it also lost three new salespeople who were dependent on the commissions from the new sales, and it lost time and money training new salespeople again. These problems could have been avoided if a portion of the sales staff had changed their attire and experimented with the results, and if an assessment had been done sooner.

Getting feedback about your progress is important from both a big picture standpoint, and a details standpoint. The big picture is the final goal you're after, for example, to lose 30 pounds in six months. The details are the smaller steps you are taking daily to achieve that final goal. In order to lose 30 pounds in six months, you must lose five pounds each month, or a pound and a quarter each week. Let's assume you start a weight loss program by eating 500 fewer calories per day; at the end of the first week you have eliminated 3,500 calories, and one pound. If you are unhappy with having lost only one pound, instead of one and a quarter pounds, you may need to further reduce your calorie intake, or exercise to burn more calories.

In the "reassessment of goals" stage, take a look at what you should have done, and do it! You are not stuck in your current reality unless you choose to remain there. This is a tough concept. When things are not going the way we desire, it is easier to say, "I had no choice." It's easier to blame circumstances or others. Most of us don't realize we do have choices in everything. We choose our friends. And some of those friends take great pride in helping us sabotage our goals. How many times have you tried to lose weight only to have a friend offer you a candy bar, or suggest you can start dieting tomorrow? How many times have you tried to stop smoking only to have a friend offer you a cigarette or suggest you start smoking again because they can't take your bad mood? If all of your friends are overweight, maybe it's time to make friends with people who are slim. If all of your friends smoke, maybe it's time to find friends who don't smoke. The choice is yours. Instead of blaming others, take control.

Most of us don't hesitate to take credit when things are going well. Now is a good time to access what is going well in your life too. What have you accomplished that you are proud of? What is working in your life? If others have helped you in these accomplishments, acknowledge them. It still wouldn't have happened, however, if you had not made the choice to go after it, so give yourself credit also.

When things are not going well, take credit for that too, and then reassess your goals and try something different.

In reassessing goals, you need to determine how much progress you have made toward your goal and what still needs to be accomplished. Another quality you need is determination. Don't quit!

Behavior Seven: Don't Quit!

Successful people don't quit! That's how they got where they are. If an outcome is possible for one person, it is probably possible for you too (barring any biological or physical restrictions), but it is possible only if you don't quit. We could all learn to be more like our cosmetic consultant, Cindy. She continued to learn and she didn't give up. Today she is every bit as financially successful as Jena.

Think about it like this: we create our own

boundaries. What would happen if you had no boundaries? What if your world could be just as you dreamed? Imagine deciding you can accomplish any project. Imagine what it would be like to do something that makes you want to get out of bed each morning?

If you are 30 years old and working eight hours per day, you have approximately 35 more years to work. At 50 weeks per year, that totals 2,000 hours per year, or 70,000 hours you still have to work in your lifetime. At 40 years old, you'll probably work 25 more years. At 2000 hours per year you have 50,000 hours to work. The choice is yours. How are you going to spend those hours?

You are ultimately making the decision to continue the pursuit of your goals, or to stop, but before you decide to give up on a goal, consider this: not long ago there was no telephone, no television, no plastic, no computers, and we hadn't been to the moon. If we had continued doing things the same old way, where would we be today?

This chapter was about creating your own luck, using specific behaviors to banish your boundaries, because in reality, luck is what you create. The remainder of this book is designed to help you take the correct thoughts and behaviors to a higher level. You'll apply visualization to implement your action plan.

Before you continue, decide exactly what you would like to work on. Next, list the negative thoughts you have about changing this area of your life. Counter these thoughts with two positive thoughts. Additionally, list the exact behaviors you need to create your goal. Then develop an action plan, the steps you will need to take, daily, in order to achieve your goal. The remainder of this book is devoted to specific concerns. Each chapter works on a specific concern using visualization to help you create success. Before you continue reading or engaging in the exercises that follow, be very clear in the goal you desire.

Be careful in what you desire, you may get it!

Note to readers: Each visualization exercise has a relaxation component that begins by counting down from 10 to one. The visualization exercises also end by counting, but here we count up from one to 10.

Chapter Four

Lose Weight with Visualization

Q s a kid I was overweight, and I have struggled with weight most of my adult life. I remember one Sunday dinner at my Grandmother's house when I complained that I wanted to lose weight. Grandma scooped another mound of pasta onto my plate and said, "If you want to lose weight, stop eating so much."

Why hadn't I thought of that! Most of us know that eating less and exercising more will result in a loss of weight. It's trying to get motivated to do these things that seems to be the problem. Visualization can help motivate you to lose weight.

You don't have to be fat. Moreover, you don't have to starve in order to achieve your desired weight. I promise! However, you do have to take a good look at yourself in that dreaded mirror. Are you happy with what you see? What would you like to see instead?

Visualization is a specific strategy with specific steps. It helps you learn to attain your goals. Visualization works! I know what you're thinking, "I've tried every diet, I hate to exercise, my family sabotages my efforts to lose weight, and I have no will power." Guess what? Visualization is an effective technique for weight loss, despite your concerns and even if other weight loss attempts have failed you. But you do have to make the choice to be thinner. You have to make the choice to learn visualization, to practice visualization and to use it to achieve and maintain your desired weight. Visualization is not a diet, but it will augment your diet. It will give you the competitive edge you need to achieve. The basic assumption is that while we each have some similar diet needs, we also have unique needs that visualization can address. About now you're probably asking, "So how can this program help people with diverse needs?" This program is designed to help each person visualize and accomplish his or her own goals.

No two people have the same weight loss requirements. For example, my sister and I are the same height, are only two years apart, were raised in the same family, and ate the same foods as children. Yet Pat cannot lose weight, or maintain her weight, with the same set of exercises and eating habits that I follow. Exercises that work to tone my body do not tone Pat's body. Since each person's body is different, the visualization each person generates will be different too. With visualization, your body can increase its weight-loss potential.

Consider this case: Diane was afraid to lose

weight. She felt she would literally die if she did not continually eat. Diane weighed 210 pounds when she decided to try visualization. She lost 25 pounds in six weeks. Diane focused on ridding herself of neurotic eating behaviors, which included eating when she was bored or stressed. She also visualized herself eating healthier foods. She began reading books on healthy eating, and the more she read and educated herself and used visualization, the more convinced she became that she would **not** die by eating fewer calories. Even if you have never been thin, and even if you have no idea how to be thin, like Diane, you can achieve your goals through visual learning.

In another case, 51-year old Dean gained weight whenever he was depressed. Dean admits, "When I was going through a divorce, I just couldn't stop eating. I was depressed for months and gained 30 pounds." Dean tried several diets and joined a weight loss group, but couldn't lose more than a couple of pounds before he started gaining again. "I'd never heard of visualization," Dean said, "yet after one session I felt prepared to make the changes I needed to lose weight."

Dean lost 30 pounds and despite another bout with depression, he has managed to maintain his current weight.

Imagine for a moment what you'll be able to accomplish once you've been instructed in visualization? Imagine yourself a person who would have no trouble passing up foods that sabotage your weight loss goals. It will happen! It will happen because you are learning to use a part of your brain you may have never used, the subconscious. Visualization is a chance to imagine using behaviors that will produce weight loss. Visualization allows you to practice and produce positive changes that will affect your weight.

You are about to learn to live in a smaller body by visualizing new thoughts and behaviors. Regardless of how many times you may have failed in the past, if you use the following instructions, you will lose weight. I promise. This does not mean you should eliminate other weight loss programs if they are helping you. Visualization may be used in conjunction with what you are already doing. Nor does this mean that there is one ideal weight for you based on your height or bone structure. If you see an unwanted bulge when you look in the mirror, or if you can pinch more than an inch of skin on your body, you may have excess fat.

Before beginning your program, check with your doctor to insure there are no medical reasons you are overweight. Then purchase a notebook to keep a log of what you eat and drink. In order to begin creating visualizations that will make a difference in your weight, you first have to know exactly how you are maintaining your current weight. If you create visualizations based on the same behaviors you are currently using, you will end up in the same position you are right now ... overweight!

The weight loss log helps you determine if you are eating because you are actually hungry, or if you have turned a situation, like watching TV, into a time to eat. The weight loss log helps you decide if there are times when you can eliminate eating, or at least eat differently, or if you can eliminate the situations where you overeat. Here's an example:

Weight Loss Log

When I eat:	Breakfast	Lunch	Dinner	Snack
What I eat:	bagel and juice	candy	salad	junk
Where:	bedroom	work	home	TV
Why:	I'm hungry	bored	hungry	habit

Times I never eat: jogging, reading, in the hot tub.

Changing your eating habits will be much easier than you think with visualization, but the first step is changing your thought patterns.

Correcting Thoughts

During my research on weight loss, clients listed several thoughts that kept them from losing weight: they thought about eating when they were stressed, lonely, bored, or felt pressured to eat. They ate if they were afraid. And some people admitted to thinking if they were overweight, it would mean they were unattractive, and they believed it would keep people at a distance. These thoughts often preceded the behaviors that followed ... eating. Answer the following questions before you continue.

What thoughts precede your behavior of eating? What thoughts keep you from losing weight? For each negative thought, add two positive thoughts as a counter. If you eat when you're stressed, what thoughts could you use to counter the behavior of eating? Look at the weight loss log section labeled "times I never eat." You could plan to increase these behaviors.

Correcting Behaviors

If you absolutely cannot give up eating when you're stressed or lonely, etc., perhaps you could change what you eat during these times. Visualize eating – and enjoying these healthy snacks in moderation: air-popped popcorn seasoned with herbs, bagels, breadsticks, broth-based soups, cereals low in fat, cocoa low in sugar and fat, English muffins, fresh fruit, frozen fruit juice bars, gingersnaps, graham crackers, low-fat or nonfat frozen yogurt, milk shakes with low-fat milk and frozen fruit, pita chips and salsa, plain yogurt with fruit and cinnamon, pretzels, rye crisp or rice cakes thinly spread with peanut butter or low-fat cheese, vegetables marinated in vinegar or dipped in low-fat yogurt, and whole-wheat crackers. Imagine yourself savoring a tall, cool glass of water. The eight glasses of water daily that health experts recommend take up space in your stomach, help your body burn fat easier, and curb your appetite.

Imagine being satisfied with fewer calories daily. Your body weight is maintained when you eat the same number of calories you burn throughout the day. To lose weight, you need to eat fewer calories than you burn in a single day, or you need to exercise to burn unnecessary calories. Ideally, you will do both. To lose one pound of body fat, you need to eliminate approximately 3,500 calories. If you eliminate 500 calories per day, for a week, you have lost 3,500 calories, or one pound. That's 50 pounds in a year!

Calories come from proteins, carbohydra[t] and fats. Proteins and carbohydrates yield fou[r] calories per gram, fats yield nine calories per gram. Therefore, foods high in fat are usually high in calorie too. Imagine reducing your fat grams. Visualize yourself eating – and being satisfied with carbohydrates such as whole-grain cereals, rice, breads, pasta, beans, nuts, fruits and vegetables. These foods are low in fat, fast burning, rich in vitamins and minerals and high in bulk, which means you will feel full on fewer calories. Imagine it is easy to follow the recommended plan of three meals and two snacks daily. Imagine eating only until you feel full and eating every four hours to reduce cravings. Begin meals with soup or broth, unbuttered bread, or raw vegetables. Eat slowly so your body has time to know it is full. Eat a variety of foods in moderation. Nothing makes eating less pleasurable than having to eat foods you can't stand. You will lose weight and you will be successful if you don't give up. Falling off your plan does not mean the effort is hopeless. It simply means you overate and you have to get back on the plan.

One way to determine your calorie intake is to multiply your desired weight by 13 if you are female, and by 18 if you are male. This determines the number of calories you can intake daily. For example, if you are female and you want to weigh 120 pounds: 120 x 13 is 1,560. You can eat 1,560 calories daily to achieve and maintain the weight of 120 pounds.

The following plan is based on 1,200 calories daily. Make copies of this plan for daily use. Simply check what you eat, and once you

d the maximum amount, you are
r the day.

Healthy Eating Plan

Fats = 4 tablespoons daily of monounsaturated fats daily

Fats
Butter
Mayonnaise
Peanut butter
Canola oil
Olive oil
Olives (3)
Nuts
Avocados
Guacamole

Fruits = 2-4 servings daily
Apples, peaches, grapes, melons, oranges,
berries,
Bananas (1/3 = a serving)
Fruit juice ½ cup= a serving

Protein = 2 - 4 servings daily
Meat and poultry and fish (1 ounce = 1
serving)
Low fat milk (6 oz.)
Cottage cheese (2 oz.)
Egg (1)

Vegetables = 3 servings daily (½ cup = 1 serving)
Lettuce
Green peppers
Asparagus
Celery
Broccoli
Cauliflower
Green beans
Spinach
Brussel sprouts
Eggplant
Kale
Squash
Carrots, corn, peas = one serving per week

Carbohydrates = 8 servings per day (1 serving = ½ cup)
Rice
Pasta
Bread (one slice = one serving)
Cereal
Potatoes (baked or boiled)
Desserts

Half of the wo:
in this country have
destined to fail are lo
none. Take a mom
behaviors you plan tc
will you eat, where w
you eat, how mar
Visualization will wo
and adopt a healthy
mind, take ten minute

the following visualization script. Eventually, you will have memorized the script. You'll become more proficient with the technique over time, and you will enjoy it more as you become proficient. Once you have reached your weight loss goal, continue practicing the visualization techniques, and search for new ways to apply the techniques and take control of your life.

Weight Loss Script

Think for a moment, how is it possible to know what to do, and not do it? *Answer the following two questions before you continue reading: What thoughts will keep you from acting the way you desire? What will keep you from losing weight?* Relax for a moment. While you're relaxing, imagine the muscles in your feet and ankles are beginning to soften, can you feel it? Just allow it to happen. We are all most comfortable doing things the way we always have. Until you have the opportunity to practice the thoughts and behaviors you desire of yourself, attaining your goals may seem difficult, or as easy as making the muscles in your lower calves begin to relax. Imagine a warm feeling moving up your legs and relaxing the muscles as you read. As the warmth es over your knees, the thigh muscles become ed. You are making the choice to relax more ore. For a few minutes, you are going to opportunity to look into your future and coming and being the person you ore you believe you are capable of rson you desire, the more you will way consistent with achieving your desires.

Right now, you are capable of allowing that warm feeling to slither into your lower abdominal and your stomach, and notice the control you have over relaxing these muscles. Allow the warmth and relaxation to deepen as it moves into your chest and along your arms. Have you noticed that each time you exhale, you are becoming more and more comfortable and relaxed. The muscles all the way down to your fingertips are beginning to feel like a limp, wet rag. Allow the warmth to move across your shoulders, into your neck and lower jaw, and across your checkbones. Feel the muscles around your eyes and across your forehead relax. As the relaxation moves over your head, your entire body feels more comfortable and more relaxed.

While you enjoy this feeling, imagine for a moment how you want to look at your desired weight. Picture yourself thinner; relax with this image. Imagine it will be as easy to achieve as it was for you to relax as you continue reading. As you read, begin to count from 10 down to one, and imagine yourself relaxing even more with each number. Ten, nine, remember that you are always in control, you will relax as much as you desire. Think for a moment of one reason that you want to lose weight. How will you look and feel when you reach your desired weight. Picture yourself. Imagine you will reach your desired weight as easily as you are able to relax yourself now. Keep this image in mind. *Before you continue, please write down your desired weight. Be reasonable. If you are in your thirties, forties or fifties, dreaming of the body that you had at fifteen years old is not reasonable.* Relax again, and notice how much more relaxed you become with number eight and seven, and for a moment can you imagine yourself standing on one side of a river bank ... imagine a river bank ... it's very beautiful, peaceful. And as you count from six down to five you may begin to notice the sounds of the river, the rushing water makes you feel comfortable. Four, three, imagine it. Imagine a warm breeze blowing across your face, two and one, notice the river water spraying as it rushes against large boulders.

Some place on the other side of that river is the person you want to become. Only the rushing water and large boulders stand between you and the other side of the river. How many boulders are there? Can you count them as you imagine yourself preparing to cross the river? Relax with the idea of making it across the river, despite any obstacles. *What is the obstacle? What thoughts keep you from losing weight? Please write out the answer now, before you continue.* Focus on your breathing for a moment; with each exhale become more comfortable. You may have noticed that the air you exhale feels warm, and the warmth is very relaxing. Imagine what will happen when you make it to the other side of the river and begin your journey from a new perspective.

Imagine the sun shining down on the other side of this river. Everything you want is on the other side. As you begin to cross the river, notice that the riverbank you are leaving has a cloud beginning to hover over it. It's getting darker. The further you move away, the darker it appears. And as you continue to move away you can no longer hear any sounds, and even the color is more difficult to see. Whatever you did on that side of the river is hard to imagine now, it's a distant past. Yet as you move toward the other side of the river, you can hear birds chirping, and see bright colored bushes. It's paradise. Everything you want is awaiting you.

Take a moment now to think about the items listed in your weight loss log. Imagine being able to eliminate just one snack, and imagine the positive thoughts you'll have when you have accomplished this. Imagine going into this same room where you usually snack but notice there is a different feeling. You desire healthy eating. There is a powerful feeling knowing you have control over when you will eat, and what you will eat. *What snack have you eliminated?* (Please write this down.)

You may choose to eliminate visiting the room you snacked in too, or the person(s) you shared this snack time with. Is this possible? Imagine what it would be like. *What positive feelings and thoughts are associated with using this behavioral strategy?* Write it down. *What could you do instead of snacking? Imagine using a new behavior, and please write down that behavior now, before you continue.*

Imagine going through your day making healthy food choices. What will you eat for breakfast, for lunch, for dinner? What will you do during your snack time? See yourself going through this day, eating healthy. How do you feel with this behavioral choice? What are you telling yourself about this choice? Consider only the positive thoughts of this choice. Any negative thoughts must be countered with two positive thoughts. Write your thoughts down.

When you have considered how you will adjust when you eat, where you eat, what you can eliminate, and the positive feelings associated with this change, imagine you are holding these changes in your right hand. Make a fist so you don't lose them.

Now take a moment and consider one negative aspect that may keep you from reaching the other side of the river with these changes still in hand. That's it, look deep into the water and find one obstacle, one negative aspect that concerns you about reaching the other side. Even if you have trouble finding it, imagine what it might be. What will keep you from becoming the person you desire? Imagine you have captured this negative aspect in your left hand. Imagine it now!

Now pause for a moment and enjoy the rushing water while you take a look at that negative aspect you're holding onto. Imagine for a moment that this negative thought is as much a figment of your imagination as the river you have pictured. Because you have imagined it, you can imagine letting it fall into the rushing water; just let it go. Open your hand and let it go. Let the water's current wash it away.

Continue to relax, your right hand is still in a fist while you continue crossing the river. Now, when the first boulder gets in your way, what will you do? How will you handle this obstacle? Focus on your fist and the positive thoughts and behaviors that will help you work your way around any obstacles. *List three ways to overcome obstacles to your weight loss.*

You are about to reach the other side and

allow your journey to begin from a new perspective. From this moment on, you will never be at this spot in the river again. You may return to the river at any time you choose, enjoy its peace and relaxation and the power that the water has at overcoming obstacles. Yet, even when you are not at the river, you may notice a peaceful feeling overcoming you whenever an obstacle gets in your way. You can handle obstacles as easily as you can relax here.

Imagine reaching the other side of this river and stepping onto the sandy banks. Something is very different here. You're not sure what it is just yet, but it goes beyond its beauty. Here you feel calm, a sense of accomplishment, because you have taken a positive step in your journey.

Here is the person you desire, step into this reality. You are this thinner person. How do you look now? How do you act? What do you think about during your day? Begin to act, think, and feel like a thinner person. You are this person, and your body has no choice but to become your vision. It will happen!

Now the journey must continue in reality. It will work if you continue to use it; don't give up. Begin counting from one up to 10. While you count, imagine gaining a greater sense of control. One, two, preparing to leave the river; three and four, but bringing with you the sense of calm, and notice that on five and six the sounds from the room you are in are more noticeable; seven and eight, nine and ten.

Weight Maintenance

Once you've reached your ideal weight, slowly increase the number of calories you consume so that your are eating the same number of calories your body is burning. If you begin to gain weight, simply reduce the calories until you lose your weight. Use the following visualization script weekly for maintenance.

Weight Maintenance Script

Once again, take a relaxing position. Just allow the muscles throughout your body to become as relaxed as possible. Imagine you are preparing for another step in your journey.

Perhaps you've already begun to realize that there is a power within you. That power is what helps you relax when you do this exercise. Begin counting to yourself as you read. You can relax more and more as you slowly count from ten down to one. As you count, the power within is growing. That same power is what helps you maintain your weight. Imagine that power is growing.

Imagine for a moment that you are following the river and that there is a steady decline. As you make your way down, you are becoming more deeply relaxed. While you make your way down, you have time to think. You may discover you are very proud of yourself for reading this book, for beginning this program, for sticking to it, and for not giving up on yourself. In fact, you probably deserve a reward. *What could be a reward for your accomplishment?* Think about that while you continue downward into a very relaxed state. When you reach the bottom, you will feel more relaxed than ever before. You will feel more assured than ever before that you will continue on this journey.

You may have already noticed that the more you walk along the river, the faster you will reach your final destination. The more you walk, you may have also noticed that even the hills are beginning to get easier to climb.

Walking has an ease to it, like the river that flows endlessly. Your journey is endless too. You will encounter many decisions to make along this journey, and many different routes will be available. Which route will you take? There will be some interesting sights to stop and see along the way. Enjoy yourself. Perhaps you can make this journey feel like a vacation. Feel very, very relaxed with your decision to continue this journey.

Imagine that when you look into the water, it appears you are looking into a mirror. What do you see when you look at your reflection? Have you noticed this is a magic mirror? What do you want to see? You can have what you desire.

Keep looking at yourself in that mirror. What do you desire? What do you look like? How do you feel? What positive thoughts do you have? As you continue along your journey, keep the image you desire of yourself always in sight. Focus on the positive thoughts and behaviors.

Look into that magic mirror again, and notice that your image has stepped out of the mirror and is heading down the river. Follow your own image. Notice the image is walking faster, yet you can easily keep up.

How do you act following your new image? *What will you eat today? How far will you walk today? Please write the answers to these questions before you continue.* You may decide to try some different routes in your daily routine, but if it doesn't work, simply try an alternate route. Maintaining your weight will be easier than you imagined.

Imagine how you and your new image will handle obstacles. You already know how. How will you reward yourself now? Write down *three rewards that are not food related.* If you are not happy with a solution toss it aside. Try another solution.

What will you do if you gain five pounds back? Write your plan out now. You've lost five pounds before; you can do it again. You may instinctively know what to do, but stop and write it out anyway. There is a strong tendency to follow plans that we have set out. Do not eliminate this step.

Imagine that you are still moving forward on your journey. Even when you catch your image, the journey continues, one day at a time. Map out your route, daily, to maintain your weight.

Walking along the river now, notice the slope is rising. The slope may look steep but imagine you can make it. How will you make it? Follow your new image; it has all the answers. If you get tired, rest, and continue when you are ready. Follow that image one step at a time, until you catch it.

For now, begin counting to yourself from one up to ten; follow the upward slope as you count. When you reach the top, you may notice a strong sense of self-fulfillment because you have set out and accomplished one goal. Read this book section again, and again, and you will maintain your weight loss goals too. When you are ready, begin your journey into reality.

Chapter Five

Stop Smoking with Visualization

*A*fter learning he had lung cancer, and two to five years to live, Mark tried to stop smoking. Unfortunately, he died trying to quit. He was 49 years old and had been a smoker for 30 years. During his 30 years as a smoker, Mark tried to quit smoking on five occasions.

"I couldn't find the motivation to actually quit," Mark said. "I guess I never really wanted to quit."

If you can't find enough reasons of your own to quit smoking, perhaps research can help motivate you. Everyone knows that the Surgeon General's Report takes the position that cigarette smoking is the cause of increased mortality. Mortality attributable to smoking accounts for 20% of all deaths in the United States every year. The 430,000 lives claimed by smoking each year represent more than those lost to AIDS, alcohol, drug abuse, car crashes, murders, suicides and fires, combined! Debilitating diseases such as cancer, emphysema, heart disease, stroke, stomach problems, and respiratory illnesses affect up to half of all long-term smokers.

But somehow we can't act on what we know. Today, there are 49 million smokers; seventy-seven percent have tried quitting. Smokers spend $330 million yearly on patches, gums, nasal sprays and inhalers to help them quit. While there is no guarantee of success, statistics indicate that using these products for six to 12 weeks can double your chance of success compared to trying to quit cold turkey. Your chance for success improves even more if you join a stop smoking program, and increases even more if you incorporate visualization. Do not hesitate to use several means for quitting. Tobacco dependence is as powerful and encompassing as any other drug addiction. People who have recovered from alcohol, heroin, cocaine, or other dependencies say that quitting smoking is much harder. Relapse occurs most often with stressful situations, interpersonal conflict, alcohol use and negative moods.

Thoughts precede behaviors. Do you really want to quite smoking? No method will help you stop smoking unless you really want to quit.

More than one million Americans quit smoking each year. If they can quit, you can too! Their reasons for quitting include: a desire to live longer, to improve their health, to have more energy and endurance when playing sports or exercising, to stop being dependent on cigarettes, to stop spending money on cigarettes and of smelling like smoke. Others want to be here for their children or grandchildren, or to remove the barriers in personal relationships. Take a moment to decide the most important reason you want to quit smoking. Next, list the positive benefits you hope to achieve by quitting.

You can quit smoking with visualization. You may choose to stop all smoking completely once you begin this program, or you may slowly reduce your cigarette consumption. The choice is yours and will depend on how you decide to use the visualization techniques. However, you must make the choice to quit smoking, to learn visualization, to practice visualization and to use it until you achieve your goal. Visualization is not a miracle formula. It will take effort on your part, but it will work if you have a true desire to quit, and if you continue to practice the techniques offered.

Correcting Thoughts

If you can visualize yourself as a non-smoker, you can achieve it. If you've tried to quit in the past, or if this is your first time quitting, take a moment right now to list any negative thoughts you have about quitting. For every negative thought find two positive reasons you should quit anyway!

Negative Thoughts	Positive Reason to Quit
1)	
2)	
3)	
4)	

Once you've quit, remaining a non-smoker is the next hurdle, and the only method that will work is being absolutely serious about wanting to quit. I don't care how many times you have tried to quit, or have failed to quit, if you use visualization, you will be able to quit and to remain a non-smoker, for good!

Imagine for a moment what you'll be able to accomplish once you've been instructed in visualization? Imagine yourself a person who will have no trouble passing up a cigarette. You won't need a cigarette first thing in the morning, or after meals, while driving, at coffee breaks, or even when you are stressed, ever again! It will happen! It will happen because you are learning to use a part of your brain you may have never used, the subconscious. Visualization engages your imagination in an effort to produce smoking cessation.

You are about to learn to stop smoking by visualizing new thoughts and behaviors. Regardless of how many times you have failed to quit smoking in the past, if you use the following instructions, you will be able to quit. And by all means take advantage of nicotine patches or gum or other smoking cessation devices. Visualization will be most effective when used in conjunction with other smoking cessation techniques.

Correcting Behaviors

Before you begin this program, purchase a notebook to keep a log of when you smoke. In order to begin creating visualizations that will make a difference in your smoking habit, you first have to know the extent of your habit. If you create visualizations based on current behaviors, you will end up in the same position you are right now ... as a smoker! Here is an example:

Smoker's Log

When I Smoke:	After breakfast	Break	Lunch	Dinner
Where:	Kitchen	lounge	café	kitchen
Why:	Habit	habit/bored		habit/bored
How many:	2 or 3	1-2		
How often:	Chain smoking	chain	chain	chain

Times I don't smoke	Taking a shower, walking, reading

Your smoker's log will help you determine if you are smoking because you actually need the nicotine, or if another reason exists. Maybe you smoke more in social situations or out of boredom. People who have formed a habit often don't even realize they are smoking. A forty-two year old private investigator fell into this category:

"While I'm working on a case I often sit and observe for hours. After keeping the smoker's log for one week, I realized I smoked more out of boredom than out of the need for nicotine. In order to break this habit I had to first become aware of when I was smoking. My first week, I visualized only smoking when I had a need for nicotine. This eliminated all my boredom smoking. I went from three packs per day down to two."

You can choose to stop smoking all at once, or use the following smoking cessation plan:

Week One: Set a date to stop all smoking. Your stop date should be set for the fourth week of your plan. For the first week, smoke only when you need the nicotine. Track your smoking with the smoker's log. For the duration of your plan, take it easy; try to avoid situations that tempt you to smoke, like arguments. Understand that you may have mood changes, you may feel sleepier or more short-tempered, but these feelings will pass. Eating low calorie snacks, drinking plenty of water, and walking or other exercise can help reduce mood changes and the urge to smoke. Remind yourself of why you are quitting. Better yet, write your reasons down and keep them in your view. Use the visualization script (below) to help you stop smoking, and choose a smoking cessation device such as patches or gums to ease your withdrawal symptoms.

Week Two: Eliminate one cigarette every other day. Continue keeping the smoker's log. Limit where you smoke, for example, you will not smoke in your house or in your car. Buy one pack of cigarettes at a time. Reward yourself for following through on your plan by going to a movie, or enjoying a favorite meal.

Week Three: Entering your third week, continue eliminating one cigarette every other day. You can probably identify circumstances that increase your desire to smoke. Write these circumstances down. This week, visualize alternatives to smoking in these circumstances. If you find yourself smoking when you become stressed, perhaps you can visualize going for a walk instead. Instead of smoking, imagine eating carrots, having a sugar free candy, trying a relaxation technique, using a nicotine patch, or chewing gum.

This is the week to carefully consider, once again, the reasons you want to quit smoking. It takes approximately 21 days to break an old habit, and 21 days to form new habits. Visualize yourself as a non-smoker.

Week Four: Your actual stop date begins this week. Pick a specific date and begin the day tobacco free. Put away the ashtrays. Change your morning routine. If you normally drink coffee, try drinking tea or fruit juice instead. Sit in a different chair when you eat breakfast, or eat in a different room. Visualize what you will do differently and write it down so you don't forget. When you get the urge to smoke or if you feel tense, try something other than reaching for that cigarette. In spite of your best efforts, remember that relapses do occur. If you backslide and smoke, don't be concerned; just get back onto your plan by continuing to use the visualization script. Each time you read the script, you will notice how much easier it becomes for you relax. Each time you read the script, you will notice how much easier it becomes to say "no" to cigarettes. It will happen! Believe it! Visualization will work if you continue to practice it, and to review your reasons for quitting.

Stop Smoking Script

Take a comfortable position in a chair, place your feet firmly on the floor and take a deep breath. Allow yourself to relax while you read this passage. The more you continue reading, the more relaxed you may notice yourself becoming.

Imagine the muscles in your feet and ankles beginning to relax and for a moment remember what it was like to take a deep breath before you were a smoker. This may seem as easy, or as difficult as it is to allow the relaxation to move up your legs, over your knees, into your thighs. Allow yourself to relax. The choice is yours to relax more and more as you continue reading. For the next few minutes, you will have the chance to imagine yourself as a non-smoker. It will happen as easily as you imagine the relaxation spreading across your lower abdominal and into your upper body. Let your arms relax. Let your chest and shoulder muscles relax. Enjoy this feeling while you continue to read.

Can you remember a time when you were a non-smoker? How old were you? Remember taking that first drag off a cigarette? As you take a deep breath, remember what it felt like to inhale that first puff of smoke into your lungs. How did it feel? Imagine that from this moment on, each time you inhale a cigarette, it will feel like the first time that you inhaled smoke into your lungs.

Most of us would never consider taking that first cigarette if we had to do it again. Imagine this is your chance to reconsider taking that first cigarette. From here on, each cigarette is a first cigarette. The choice is yours to take it, or pass. Where were you the first time you smoked? Were you alone or with others? Was it your idea to smoke, or did someone else suggest it? Remember how you felt when taking that first drag.

While you continue to relax, imagine for a moment that you are holding that first cigarette, and bring today's knowledge into the past. Knowing what you now know, would you have taken that first drag? Imagine how easy it would have been to pass that cigarette up. Just put it down. Just say "no" each time you are tempted from here on.

As you continue reading, stop and count from ten down to one. With each number, allow yourself to relax even more, and notice that with each number your confidence level increases. You will be able to say "no" to each cigarette. Imagine it will happen as easily are you were able to relax while reading this passage. Stop, and count now.

Pause for a moment and think about one reason that you want to become a non-smoker. How will you look when you have accomplished your goal to be a non-smoker? How will it feel? Imagine a light feeling. Imagine that being a non-smoker will make everything in your life feel easier to accomplish. Life will seem like an extended vacation.

Perhaps you can imagine traveling in a deluxe train car across the country. Imagine standing in the train station waiting for your trip to begin. Maybe you've taken a train trip before. However, imagine this destination will be different. In fact, you don't know when this trip will end, and you don't care. Imagine that. No matter where this trip takes you, or how it ends, it will be an enjoyable experience.

Notice that as you enter the train car you become more and more comfortable about taking this trip. While preparing to leave the train station, sit back in your seat and take a deep breath to relax even more. It is nice to let someone else do the driving. Look out the window of the train. The people waving the train off are all smoking cigarettes. In fact, they are smoking so much that it is becoming difficult to see them through the gray haze. As the train begins to pull away from the station, notice the smoke is filling the scene and darkening your view. You can hear a faint coughing and now, for the first time you can see why everyone is waving their hands. They are not really waving good-bye to the train; they are waving the smoke away from their faces. The color in the station is becoming dimmer as you pull away. It feels good to be pulling away.

Looking ahead, you can see beautiful blue skies. The train is picking up speed and the trees are rushing past your window. There is a gentle rocking as the train moves along the track. It's comforting to know that you can by-pass any stop and continue to the next station. Or you can stop any time you desire. Each stop brings new things to see and learn. At one of these stops, you will fully discover yourself as a non-smoker. It is an easily attainable desire. How many stops you make is up to you, but the trip does not end until you have reached your final destination. Imagine what will happen when you reach your final destination and your life begins from a new perspective.

The station you've left behind already seems distant. As you continue to move toward a new destination, a level of anticipation and excitement overcomes you. Although you can leave this train whenever you desire, you must continue until the next stop. Perhaps you have noticed this is a smoke-free train. Are you afraid you can't make it until the next stop?

What can you do to occupy your time until the next stop? Imagine you will become so engrossed in the scenery that the time until the next stop is whizzing by like the trees outside your window. The trees are a blur passing your window. Time can be a blur too. It can pass as easily as the trees you have noticed. Imagine it! Imagine what behaviors will help your time pass?

You are on a vacation that is leaving the smoke-filled station behind. It is a most interesting thought to consider that you never have to return here. If you find a stop along the way that you enjoy, you can stay as long as you desire. Alternatively, you can continue the journey, learning and enjoying what life has to offer you from a new perspective. You feel powerful knowing that you have control over which stops to take. You can remain at any stop, or get back on the train and continue the trip. The choice is yours.

The choice is also yours to remain in this train car, or to explore other cars. What would happen if you left this train car? What do the other cars have to offer that you may be missing by staying here? Go ahead; imagine moving toward the next car. Your footing may feel a bit wobbly with the gentle rocking motion of the train, but you can make it. After all, you want to see what's in that next car.

Aliens from galaxies unknown are in the next car, yet they appear to know each other. They're mingling around talking with each other, laughing, and when you get closer, they invite you to join them. They appear different to you, but you don't appear different to them. It may seem a bit uncomfortable to you at first because the differences go beyond their looks, but it is not unbearable; it's just different. What do you do in this situation? Observe the aliens. What do they do? Observe them. Imitate them. Do they walk differently than you do? Do they have a different attitude than you do? Perhaps they have a confidence that you are not feeling yet. Notice that they don't seem to be wobbling to the rocking motion of the train car. Perhaps they are used to the motion of the train. Imagine that you are becoming used to the motion of the train too. How would you walk if you knew you would feel at ease? Try walking, and if an alien person gets in your way, imagine walking confidently past, as if you've been on this train for a lifetime.

You may find yourself truly enjoying this trip. Even the parts of the trip you were unsure of may become enjoyable. Imagine that! Now the train is approaching its first stop, and your journey must continue in reality. You can return to this train at any time you desire simply by re-reading this passage. Eventually, you will have this passage memorized and you may notice that the more you practice, the more quickly your body will relax. Begin counting to yourself, from one up to ten. With each number, feel a greater sense of confidence in yourself and a greater control over your situation. Move toward reality with an urgency to begin your trip from a new perspective. Allow it to happen.

Smoking Maintenance

Once you have completely stopped smoking, use the following visualization script for maintenance. Any time you feel compelled to smoke, read the maintenance script immediately. If you have no urge to smoke, read this section weekly for the first six months after smoking cessation.

Stop Smoking Maintenance Script

Think for a moment. What might cause you to smoke again? Relax and think about this for a moment. While you're thinking, imagine the muscles in your feet and ankles are beginning to relax. Can you feel it? Just allow it to happen. We are all most comfortable doing things the way we always have. Until you have the opportunity to practice the behavior you desire of yourself, it may seem difficult, or as easy as making the muscles in your lower calves begin to relax. Imagine a warm feeling moving up your legs and relaxing the muscles as you read. As the warmth goes over your knees, the thigh muscles become relaxed. You are making this choice to relax more and more. For a few minutes, you are going to have the opportunity to look into your future and practice being the person you desire. The more you believe that you are capable of achieving what you desire, the more you will begin to act in a way that is consistent with achieving your desires.

Right now, allow a warm feeling to slither into your lower abdominal and your stomach. Notice the control you have over relaxing these muscles. Allow the warmth and relaxation to deepen as it moves into your chest and along your arms. Have you noticed that each time you exhale, you are becoming more and more comfortable and relaxed. Allow it to happen. The muscles all the way down to your fingertips are beginning to feel like a limp, wet rag. Allow the warmth to move across your shoulders, into your neck and lower jaw, and then across your checkbones. Feel the muscles around your eyes and across your forehead relax. As the relaxation moves over your head, your entire body feels more comfortable and more relaxed.

While you enjoy this feeling, imagine for a moment how wonderful it feels to breathe as a non-smoker. Imagine it will be as easy for you to remain a non-smoker as it is for you to relax while you continue reading. Begin to count from 10 down to one, and imagine yourself relaxing even more. Ten, nine, remember that you are always in control. You can relax as much as you desire, or stop this exercise at any time you desire. Think for a moment of one reason that you want to remain a non-smoker? Imagine it will happen as easily as you are able to relax. Notice how much more relaxed you become with the numbers eight and seven, and for a moment imagine you are back on the train. Look out the window; it's very beautiful, peaceful. And as you count to six and five, you may begin to notice the sounds of the train rolling along the track and allow the sound to help you relax. Four, three, imagine it; listen to the sounds, two and one, feel the gentle rocking of the train.

In the distance there is a mountain. Some place along this mountainous route the strength you feel as a non-smoker will intensify. Distance is all that stands between you and the other side of the mountain. The mountain peaks may be blocking your view and making it impossible for you to see how far you must travel. Can you prepare to cross the mountain? Relax with the idea of making it across the many peaks and valleys. Focus on your breathing for a moment; each time you exhale notice you are becoming more comfortable. You may have noticed that the air you exhale feels warm, and the warmth is very relaxing. Imagine what will happen when you make it to the other side of the mountain and begin your journey from a new perspective.

Now you are going into a tunnel. Everything you want is on the other side of this tunnel. As you travel into the tunnel, notice how everything begins to darken. It's getting darker. The further you move into the tunnel the darker it appears until it is almost black. Whatever you did before entering this tunnel has a blackened image too. It's a distant past. Yet as you move through the tunnel to the other side of the mountain and emerge into the light, you can see bright colored bushes. It's paradise. Everything you want is awaiting you. Take a moment and imagine how easily you can achieve what you desire.

Hold on to this thought. Make a fist with your right hand and hold on to this thought. Now take a moment and consider one negative aspect that may keep you from reaching the other side of this mountain. That's it; find one negative aspect that concerns you about remaining here. Even if you have trouble finding it, imagine what it might be. What troubles you? Imagine you have captured this negative aspect in your left hand. Imagine it now! If you're not sure what it is, guess.

Now pause for a moment and enjoy the train ride while you take a look at that negative aspect you are holding onto. Imagine for a moment that this negative aspect is as much a figment of your imagination as the train you have pictured.

Because you have imagined it, you can imagine opening the window and letting the negative aspect float away with the wind. Open your left hand and let it go. Let the wind blow it away.

Continue to relax. Your right hand is still in a fist while you continue your trip. Now, when any negative aspect gets in your way, what will you do? How will you handle it? Focus on what you hold in your closed fist and work your way around any obstacles.

Enjoy the peace and relaxation and the power of your own thoughts and behaviors. Yet, even when you are not at the mountains, you may notice that a peaceful thought is always within your reach.

Imagine the train has stopped. Step off the train and onto the gentle slopes. You are on top of the world looking down. Something is very different from this perspective. You may not know what it is, but it goes beyond its beauty. There is a sense of accomplishment that is peaceful and fulfilling.

Now the journey must continue in reality. Visualize your success. Visualization will work if you continue to use it. Don't give up. Begin counting from one up to ten. Move toward reality with a sense of greater control, and an urgency to begin, one, two, three and four, bringing with you the sense of calm, and notice that on five and six the sounds from the room you are in are more noticeable. On seven and eight you can feel a confidence you have never experienced; on nine and ten begin your trip into reality.

Chapter Six

Toning and Exercising Your Body with Visualization

Get motivated to workout, burn fat, shape up, and tone that body! It can happen with visualization. Anyone who is interested in looking great knows that it goes beyond diet and nutrition. We also need an exercise plan to get our bodies into shape.

At only five feet tall, Joanne weights 123 pounds. However, she is 123 pounds of pure muscle. Muscle weighs more than fat. "I used to weigh 123 pounds of pure fat," Joanne said. "Every part of my body jiggled when I walked. I had a roll of fat on my stomach and you wouldn't have caught me dead in a bathing suit. Today, I look great at the same weight. I exercise and I enjoy it, thanks to visualization."

If you can imagine yourself in great shape, you can achieve it! Visualization can help you get motivated to begin an exercise program, and to stick with it. I can already hear what you're saying: "I've tried every exercise program. I have a shelf of books on how to exercise and a basement full of unused exercise machines." And you probably have no motivation to exercise. Visualization can actually help you begin to enjoy exercising, but you have to make a choice to practice the visualization techniques, daily. Sound simple? It is. Sound too good to be true? It isn't. You still have to do the work; you still have to exercise.

With visualization you choose the exercise you desire (some of you are saying "no exercise is what I desire.") So let me re-phrase that sentence to read, "Some of you may want to choose the exercise that is the least offensive." There are no gyms to join, and no workout schedules to maintain, unless you choose this option. Do what works best for you ("no exercise" is not an acceptable answer). This program is designed to help each person visualize and accomplish their own needs and exercise goals.

Whatever exercise regime you choose, generating positive mental images can help you learn to enjoy exercising. Consider Jeannie's story.

"I began by visualizing just one new action. I visualized beginning my day with fifteen minutes of walking. The minute I got out of bed in the morning I immediately went for my walk. If I tried to walk later in the day, I found every excuse not to walk. When I retired for the evening, I visualized getting out of bed the next morning and walking. I imagined how good it would feel to enjoy the fresh morning air, and how much more energy I would have for starting my day."

Jeannie felt relaxed, in control and alert. Within two months she was walking 30 minutes daily. She enjoyed how she felt while walking, and she enjoyed that her body was becoming toned.

"Before practicing visualization, I had tried, and quit, almost every exercising program," Jeannie said. "I belonged to a gym that I attended for three weeks, I took karate, judo, ballroom dance lessons, jazz dance, jazzercise, weight training, tennis, racquetball, horseback riding lessons, swimming, aerobics, walking and jogging. All were undertaken with the idea of keeping some part of my body in shape. I was an exercise failure. I wanted to find an exercise program I could stick with and feel motivated to continue purely because it felt good and my body was getting into shape. Visualization was my answer."

Visualization works, which is why 80 % of top athletes use it as part of their training. Notice I said "as part of their training." Muscles must be worked to get them in shape, which means you have to exercise. Using visualization alone will not get your muscles into shape.

So what type of workout should you do? Aerobics is the most common way to get rid of fat. This can include running, bicycling, jumping rope, and aerobic dance. While these exercises will burn fat and keep the heart and lungs healthy, they do not re-shape sagging body parts; adding weights to your workout routine builds muscle and re-shapes your body. Simply put, when you increase the amount of muscle you have, your resting metabolic rate goes up. Therefore, while you may have burned 80 calories an hour just sitting, you now burn approximately 100-120 calories per hour doing the same thing. So exercising and building muscle helps you maintain your weight. Unfortunately there are no short cuts. Your progress depends upon you.

Obviously, if you are overweight, you'll want to read the section on weight loss and use it in conjunction with exercising. Otherwise, you'll build muscle, but you may have fat on top of the muscle.

Correcting Thoughts

Before you begin, I'd like you to list every negative thought you have about getting into shape:

1)
2)
3)
4)
5)
6)
7)
8)
9)
10)

For each negative thought, balance it with two positive thoughts on why you want to get into shape. Some of your thoughts might include having failed in the past (I won't fail again), feeling you don't have time to workout (I will make time to workout), considering yourself a basically lazy person (I have a lot of energy), or maybe you feel too overweight to workout (I'll start out slowly).

Mental attitude counts when it comes to achieving your desired goal. Many studies have shown that people with positive attitudes recover from operations faster, and have fewer complications from surgery, and generally get along better in life. The mind has many powers that can not be explained. How is it people can undergo surgery or dental procedures with no anesthesia? First, they believe they can do it. Without a belief that it is possible to achieve your goals, it can not happen.

Bob was 100 pounds overweight when I met him. It took him one year to lose weight and re-shape his body. "I've lost weight before," Bob said, "but usually I was flabby afterwards. I decided to visualize myself not only losing weight, but also toning my body. I started walking one mile each day. After I'd lost 25 pounds I decided to add weight training to re-shape my body. I could not believe the difference when I reached my ideal weight. I had pictures of myself when I had lost weight in the past, and I could still see a roll of fat under my shirt. This time, at the same weight, the roll of fat was gone, and I could actually see muscle instead!"

Jill had fifty pounds to lose. "It was gone in twenty-five weeks. However, even after losing 25 pounds, my body was so toned that I looked slimmer than I did when I weighed the same weight before. I decided to lose 40 pounds instead of the 50 I had originally intended to lose."

Recently I decided to tone up. I added light weights to my daily 30-minute jog. It took me approximately six weeks to begin noticing a difference. I do three sets of 20 repetitions for my arms and legs, every day. It is not a demanding exercise schedule; however, when I looked in the mirror I saw a dramatic difference.

If you're just trying to tone your body, it will take approximately six to 10 weeks before you'll notice results. Don't be surprised if you gain a pound or two, since muscle weighs more than fat. Whenever I've gained a few pounds I'd like to rationalize that I must have exercised more that week, not likely! But instead of letting the scale be your judge, let the mirror become your judge.

Visualization works! Simply take 10 minutes each day, use the following visualization program and you'll soon find yourself exercising and toning your body, I promise!

Visualization Script
For Toning and Exercising

Take a moment right now and begin relaxing your body. Find a comfortable position lying flat or sitting in a chair and simply allow yourself to relax. Start at your feet allowing the muscles to relax, and move the relaxation to your ankles and calves. Let the muscles in your calves loosen while you begin to imagine getting in shape. How will you actually look when you are in shape?

When you have a mental picture of yourself in shape, continue to relax your body. Allow the relaxation to move upward, over your knees and into your thighs. The choice is yours to relax more and more as you continue reading. For the next few minutes, you have the chance to imagine what life will be like when you incorporate an exercise program into your daily routine. It will happen as easily as you imagine the relaxation spreading into your hips, lower abdominal, and into your upper body. Allow your chest, shoulders, your arms, your entire body to relax. Enjoy these feelings while you continue reading.

For a moment, imagine you are a movie star with a perfect body? Who are you? How do you imagine this movie star stays in shape? Think about this while you continue to relax. Count with me from 10 down to one and with each number allow yourself to relax even more with the idea of getting into shape. Ten and nine, relaxing more and more; eight and seven, while you continue reading you may begin to notice that you are beginning to take deeper breaths. You are feeling more relaxed on six and five. Notice there is a confidence building within you. That confidence becomes stronger on the numbers four and three. Imagine how easy it will be to get your body into shape and keep it that way, and on two and one notice how easy it was for you to relax. Take a deep breath and feel every muscle relax even more as you continue reading.

Each time you read this passage, you will notice how much easier it is to relax. Each time you read this passage, you will notice it is easier to imagine yourself taking the steps to get into shape.

Think about one reason that you want to get into shape. How will you look when have accomplished this goal? How will you feel? How will you think? Imagine thinking only positive thoughts. Imagine you already have a terrific body. How will you keep this terrific body? Imagine that! How will you keep in shape? What behaviors will you use to keep in shape?

Movie stars make the time to exercise, especially when they are on location. If you could be on location, what town would you be in? Even as an in-demand movie star, making millions of dollars per movie, in order to keep your body in shape, you must continue your workouts. Imagine for a moment, you are traveling to a new location. You've spent hours on an airplane, shuffling from airport to airport before you finally land. You're tired, and you're jet lagged, but because your body is in such great shape, you have a renewed burst of energy once you reach your hotel. Since you have never been in this hotel, you have no idea what type of exercise equipment is available. You don't even know where to find the workout room, but you must find it. Being in a new place can be so frustrating. Take a deep breath and let any frustration you feel work for you rather than against you. Movie stars can't afford to let frustrations keep them from their workouts.

Imagine calling the front desk. The clerk on the phone says the workout room is located in the hotel basement. You are on the 10th floor. You could decide to take the stairs as part of your workout. Imagine heading down the stairs, and a feeling of accomplishment at having made the decision to use the stairs. You can feel your leg muscles beginning to tighten as you pick up your pace. Notice your heart pumping and a feeling of exhilaration! You can actually feel the muscles becoming toned; it feels wonderful. As you descend toward the basement workout room, the feeling of exhilaration is overwhelming. You can't wait to reach the basement. There is an excitement about trying out new equipment and new routines. When you finally reach the workout room, it is more than you could have imagined.

Its décor looks like a cave. There's a mystery about it, but it's intriguing as well. Every type of workout equipment is available. If you get tired of one routine, simply follow the caverns of the cave to another area and try another piece of equipment. And are you surprised how quickly time has passed while you are in the cave? Imagine feeling just as you do at this moment every time you exercise, relaxed, yet exhilarated, and excited.

Feel every muscle in your body as it works out, and tones up. What exercise do you like the best? There is not enough time to try them all in this session. Perhaps you'll try another tomorrow. Imagine a feeling of disappointment at having to leave this cave today. But feel assured that you can return to the cave tomorrow.

For now your workout is over. Imagine every muscle feeling toned, yet relaxed. What's interesting about this cave is that you can return here anytime you desire, from any location. You are now prepared to begin shooting your movie. You are now prepared to begin living your life like a star. Imagine it!

Begin counting from one up to ten and imagine climbing toward your room in the hotel. When you reach the top you may notice a sense of self-fulfillment because you have set out and accomplished one goal.

Toning and Exercise Maintenance Script

It's time to return to the cave. Remember

how it felt when you were last here? Go back to that same feeling of relaxation. That's it. Take in a deep breath, and feel relaxed. As you read, imagine yourself counting from ten down to one. With each number allow yourself to relax even more. Begin counting. Good. Continue to count as you read. You are becoming more and more relaxed. Just allow it to happen.

Look around the cave. You may have noticed there are several exercise options you can explore. Choose one of the options and go exploring. There is nothing to fear. There is no wrong choice but to remain where you are in this journey. Move. Walk in any direction. Imagine it. Good.

Perhaps you can imagine the challenge of following a new direction. It may feel uncomfortable, or exciting, or stressful. You may feel that you already know what the outcome will be, even though you don't know exactly what is ahead of you.

For a moment, imagine the worst. What is the worst? Imagine it. Perhaps your movie star body will begin to lose shape. Do you really have anything to fear?

Imagine you've found a treasure map, and when you find this treasure it will be the best thing that has ever happened to you. Imagine that! What is your treasure? Follow the route mapped out before you knowing that when you reach your destination, the treasure will be yours.

You know how to attain this treasure. Imagine how easy it will be for you to acquire. Maybe it will take 15 minutes of your time each day, maybe it will take 20 or 30 minutes, but you will attain it, and it will be worth the few moments of your time to acquire it.

Imagine your map has several choices outlined, several routes. Is it possible these routes can be heading in the same direction? How can that be? How can you head the same direction and achieve different outcomes? Is that possible? Think about it.

Look at your map. Perhaps now you can see that there are many routes leading to the same treasure? There are several direct routes. However, notice the other routes. Some may take longer. Some may be more scenic. Some may be more or less strenuous. There are also many routes leading to the worst destination. Even though the worst destination and the treasure destination appear to be following the same route, something is different.

It's like following a road map to your favorite vacation spot. Once you arrive, there are many options to consider. Some places will bring more pleasure than others. You must decide what is the most pleasurable. You must decide which route makes you feel and look like a movie star. And you must decide to stay away from the places that offer the worst alternatives. If you take a route that seems wrong, turn around and head in another direction. If you end up at a destination you don't like, don't stay there. Keep traveling until you find your treasure.

The treasure is there if you search for it. It is there if you don't give up. Yet there are times it seems lost in the confusion.

Look around this cave while you travel. Look deep inside. Have you encountered the rare species of animals yet? Keep walking, you'll see them. Some have been extinct for years, yet they are not to be feared. Simply enjoy that these rare species are mingling around inside. Simply be aware that they exist.

Some species are brightly colored: neon greens, blues, reds, and yellows. The colors are flashing all around you. You might be wondering just what you came in here to learn. What did you come in here to learn? The answer to this question is here. Keep looking around. Now is the time to discover that answer. After all, you are the director; you can make this movie end any way you please.

It is wonderful to be curious, to live in wonder of how things will turn out. No matter what you discover, you will feel comfortable, and relaxed, you'll be at peace with yourself and with what you find in here, because you know it's only a movie. You are the director, so you can turn around and take a different route at any time you choose. Just because you chose this route once, does not mean you must continue on this path again.

Directors often have actors do one film take after another until the perfect scene has been captured on film. Perhaps you'll change the angle of the shot; perhaps you'll change the surroundings. What are you after in this shot?

Think. If you had a question, what would it be? What are you after? The answer is here. Search for it. Find it before you decide to leave this film take. And while you are searching, notice there is a waterfall up ahead. And there are stairs leading to a sparkling pool of water below. Take one step at a time; descend toward the pool below. With each step, you may notice a feeling of confidence. You can handle anything now. You can control your outcomes. You are closer now and in a moment, you are going to touch the water, and you are going to touch on your questions and answers. Is there more than one question, or perhaps more than one answer? When you take the last step, look into the water, lean forward and touch it. Notice your reflection; notice what is different in the reflection staring back at you. Something is different.

Notice how it feels as you step into the water. The water is refreshing and it is a reminder of the ease that you can eliminate concerns. Notice how light you feel in the water, how light you feel without concerns. This is a good place to leave your concerns. Imagine how much easier your journey will be without concerns. When you get what you need from the pool of water, it is time to continue the journey.

The choice is yours. If you must take along concerns, imagine they are a ball and chain tied to your ankle. You are the actor. With each step imagine the ball is being dragged behind you, and imagine the anguish on your face. You will still make your destination, but it will seem more difficult. Since you are directing this movie, the choice is yours. At any time you choose you can cut the chain and go on without the concern dragging you down. Take a deep breath and imagine how life will feel with no concerns to drag you down or hold you back.

Look at your treasure map and make a decision. Which direction shall you follow? With your map in hand, begin today's journey. You have a very specific destination. As the director, instruct yourself to act confidently. Imagine there is nothing to keep you from reaching your goal. As you climb back up the stairs and continue along the cave route, notice a stream of sunlight is guiding you. You have a bright future ahead as you begin counting to yourself. Begin with one. As you continue counting up to ten, imagine beginning your next journey. Imagine each journey will bring with it a feeling of relaxation, and confidence. And when you are ready, you may continue this journey in reality.

Chapter Seven

Reduce Stress with Visualization

Most of us associate stress with the negative events that happen in our lives. Perhaps you have a work project due and your computer has just crashed. You have a job interview and your car won't start. A water pipe in your home has started leaking. Your kids have been home ill for a week, and now you're sick.

Rarely do we consider that stress can also be associated with the positive events that happen in our lives. You're going on a first date with someone you've been attracted to for months, and you're hoping it will lead to a second date. Your new business has taken off and you hope you can fill the orders. You've just sold your house, but you haven't found a new one.

The problem is that our bodies can't tell the difference between negative or positive stress. It simply reacts. The reactions we have to stress are our body's way of alerting us to danger. This can include an increased respiratory and heart rate, headaches, fatigue, and rising blood pressure. However, if we don't learn to manage stress in healthy ways, the stress can cause health-related problems. A study of hundreds of heart attack victims showed that a handful had actually been promoted the previous week.

This may explain why students, after an intense period of studying for midterms, are often sick on spring break. A number of studies have shown that the process of continuous stress depresses our immune system. A week after a stressful event you'll have a cold.

Take a moment right now and list everything that causes stress in your life. Next to each item that causes you stress, list how you usually handle that stress.

Stress Log

Causes of Stress   **Reaction to Stress**

1)
2)
3)
4)
6)
7)
8)
9)
10)

The tendency under stressful circumstances might be to smoke a cigarette, overeat, get drunk, gamble, or to go shopping.

These are a few of the negative ways we often deal with stress. Since positive and negative stresses are part of everyone's life, we need strategies to manage it more effectively. Visualization can help.

Correcting Thoughts

If you can imagine developing positive thoughts for reducing stress, you can achieve it! Visualization works. Several years back when Nancy was going through a divorce, she was so stressed that she developed a skin rash. She saw a dermatologist and was prescribed cortisone to help the rash, but the rash returned the minute she discontinued the medication. This routine went on for six months until she tried visualization. It worked! "Within two weeks, the rash disappeared and it has never returned," Nancy said. "I simply take time to relax now. The relaxation component of visualization is so enjoyable that I focus on this aspect."

Dawn instantly became stressed when she decided to return to college for an advanced degree. As if college were not enough, she was working full-time, and had three teenagers she was raising by herself. Dawn took ten minutes each morning to imagine going through her day with thoughts of excitement, energy, and the delight of learning something new each day. She couldn't wait for each new day to begin in wonder of what it might bring. Life became a fascinating journey for her just by developing positive thoughts.

For each negative thought you have today, list at least two positive thoughts to counter it, and stay focused on the positive.

Correcting Behaviors

If you can make strong mental pictures of what you want while affirming to yourself that you can and will get it ... you will get it! It will take a commitment of ten minutes, each day, for you to use visualization. In addition to changing negative thoughts, you may want to consider reducing any negative behaviors you use for handling stress.

The first negative behavior you can eliminate is using caffeine. When you're stressed, drinking just two cups of coffee, or sodas with caffeine, can increase the adrenaline in your bloodstream. At a time when your body is already producing more adrenaline than it can deal with, caffeine may result in a lack of concentration. However, if you're used to drinking two cups of coffee per day, eliminating all caffeine may produce a withdrawal system, such as a headache. Begin with a gradual reduction of caffeine.

Second, eliminate sugar. Sugar will boost your energy level temporarily, then bring you down hard causing fatigue. Since stress often causes fatigue, sugar will aggravate the fatigue.

Third, increase your exercise. When you're stressed, the body has a "fight or flight" reaction. Epinephrine and norepinephrine pour out, causing your heart to race and the blood pressure to rise in preparation for a physical threat. This reaction is great if you have to run from a mugger, but it isn't the best way to handle slow traffic. Exercising burns off the excess chemicals that have been created by stressful situations and this helps calm you down. Aerobic activities such as walking, jogging, swimming, biking, etc., for 30 to 40 minutes every day will work wonders for reducing stress.

Fourth, laughter can have an anesthetic effect because it stimulates endorphins. Additionally, laughter has been shown to give patients several hours of pain-free sleep. Visualize doing things that can increase your laughter and joy in life. Go to a comedy club, read joke books, spend more time with friends or family you enjoy, go to a movie.

Fifth, focus on the positive. When I saw the movie *City of Angels* one line stuck in my mind: "What did you like most about living?" I now write in a journal daily to list what I like about life. The journal helps me keep focused on the positive things about life.

Look at your Stress Log again. What options listed above could you incorporate into your daily routine to eliminate stress? Obviously, the suggestions listed above can be used alone; however, in conjunction with visualization, they can increase your chance of successfully reducing stress from your life. I think you'll also enjoy the feeling of relaxation that visualization brings. I suggest you practice these exercises twice a day for reducing stress.

Visualization Script For Reducing Stress

Take a comfortable position in a chair, both feet on the floor and begin to relax. Imagine you are reading this book while preparing to take a walk into the woods. It's a beautiful warm and sunny day and the birds are chirping. Begin to relax as you count to yourself from 10 down to one. With each number you count allow yourself to relax even more. When you have finished counting, focus on a warm feeling moving from your feet upward, the more the warmth moves up the more you relax. Feel the warmth in your calves and allow it to spread over your knees and across your stomach. Allow the muscles to simply relax as you read. Feel the relaxation as the warmth moves into your chest, and with each breath you take allow the relaxation to double. You are beginning to feel like a limp wet rag as the warmth moves into your arms, across your shoulders, into your neck and all the way over your head. Your cheek muscles, the muscles across your forehead and your eyebrows feel like they are relaxing. You may notice an increasing sense of calm overcoming you.

Right now, imagine you are going on a journey. You're going to follow a winding path into the woods and enjoy a day of peace and tranquility, and nature. As you are beginning, notice there is a stick stuck in the mud and it's blocking your path. It's a large stick, but notice how easy it is to remove when you tug on it. Toss it aside and begin your journey. This path goes in a circle, but where you begin is not where you will end. What happens along the path to make things appear different is up to you, despite that you end up right back where you started. How is that possible?

Any time you begin a journey you must decide what you will take along. What do you need for today's trip? Imagine putting these items into a backpack. Each day when you take this journey, you can fill your backpack again.

With your backpack filled, imagine putting it over your shoulders now. Imagine that it feels very, very heavy. The straps feel like they are cutting into your shoulders? Can you imagine how uncomfortable it will be to carry this along the river all day? Your shoulder muscles are beginning to ache. Feel the tension pulling all the way into your neck and lower jaw and throughout your entire body. It is very, very uncomfortable. You may even be noticing your shoulder muscles beginning to cramp and that you have an uncontrollable urge to get rid of the backpack, despite the fact that you feel you need these items for this trip.

Try dragging the backpack instead. Go ahead, grab hold of the straps and just pull the backpack along. Take a few steps and notice how you're walking bent over now, and the backpack drags in the rocks and sand along the path making it seem even heavier. You may have even noticed the backpack strap cutting into your hand. Imagine it feeling very uncomfortable; it's holding you back. Something has to come out of this backpack. What can you eliminate to make this journey more comfortable? Imagine you simply can't take another step until you've resolved this problem.

Think for a moment. Why are you here? What do you want from this journey? How will you get it? What positive thoughts do you have? What behaviors will you use? What can you eliminate from your backpack to make this journey more comfortable? Once your backpack is ready, begin to follow the path into the woods, again. Deeper into the dense wooded area, feel a sense of comfort knowing that you are moving in the right direction. After all, how can you make a wrong turn when you are following a circular path? Allow your entire body to relax, more and more relaxed, one step at a time, slowly moving into the woods.

The terrain along this path is flat and very easy for you to handle, and if you begin to feel worn down, stop and rest. Imagine yourself sitting down and allowing yourself to simply relax. Enjoy sitting down calmly. And when you are ready, begin again, slowly working toward your destination. If you continue the journey, you will reach that destination. And if you walk, you won't become so winded. Take your time, but don't give up.

Imagine that you've been walking and resting for several hours, and you may have even noticed that your breathing is heavier and your body has a feeling of stimulation. You can actually sense a tingle overcoming you. Like the muscles are pushing all of the toxins out of your body. You've never felt anything quite like it before. Imagine something is happening to your body. It's a good feeling, but different.

Then you hear it, a rustling in the trees. But you can't see anything. Find a resting spot to observe. You are waiting but nothing is happening. Or is something happening? Can you feel it? The tension, the silence. Something is out there; you are sure of it, but what?

While you wait you may want to reach for that backpack. What did you bring along that could ease this tension? This waiting? Imagine reaching for a positive thought or behavior. Something has to change and it must start with you. Maybe you'll simply decide to start walking again; leave your troubles behind. What other behaviors could work for you?

Continue your journey with a renewed assurance that you will make it. You will not give up. Imagine whenever you feel you can't make it that you simply start walking. You can walk no matter where you are. You can use whatever behaviors work. What works?

The next time you need a break and look into that backpack, what will you find? Take a break and imagine that now. In addition, each day when you fill your backpack for the day's journey, what will you fill it with? The choice is yours.

And the journey continues. Someplace along this journey you will find the person you are looking for. As long as the journey continues, you are one step closer to reaching that goal. Perhaps you have already noticed that each step helps you become more relaxed and more assured that you will reach that goal. How far you travel each day is up to you, but keep heading in the same direction. There is only one path, and it continues to circle around.

Perhaps you can imagine the relaxation and assurance you will feel when you have traveled the full circle. Although you are back at the beginning, something very significant has occurred. Something you will not forget as you begin your next journey in reality. Begin counting from one up to 10. One, two, three, your breathing becomes more normal and you are noticing the sounds outside of this room. Four, five, prepare to start this journey with renewed enthusiasm, six, seven, eight, nine, and ten.

Reduce Stress Maintenance Script

Once again, take a comfortable position and notice that you may already be more relaxed than the last time you began this exercise. Count from 10 to nine and just as before, your feet and ankles feel a warmth that is comforting. You are very relaxed as you continue to count from eight to seven and allow the warmth to move upward into your calves; allow the muscles to loosen; loosen them even more; more, that's it. Six and five allow the relaxation to spread over your knees and into your thighs. You are more and more relaxed as it moves upward and reaches your abdominal. Allow that warmth to continue upward on four, and three, your chest muscles and shoulders are becoming limp. Feel the relaxation spread all the way down your arms and into your fingertips, relaxing more and more. Notice that your breathing has become deeper and your entire body, your neck and head feel more relaxed than ever before. On two, and one, your entire body relaxes even more, more, as you imagine returning to the woods.

You can walk through the woods, or you may quicken the pace. Have you noticed what a relaxed feeling you have knowing that you control the pace. You are in control of all of your thoughts and behaviors. Some of these behaviors are new. Maybe you'll decide to get off of the circular path today, and explore the woods before you. What will you find? Are you nervous, are you excited? Imagine this is your first time off of the circular path.

You walk deeper and deeper into the woods. Many obstacles block your path, but you push right past them. For the first time, you notice a river up ahead. You had no idea it existed. And there's a rowboat. It is awkward to maneuver a rowboat the first time you are in one. Go ahead, get inside, feel it rocking as the water ripples beneath. Let yourself begin to drift along with the current until suddenly a boulder appears to be getting in your way. And there's a moment of panic when you realize you are headed into a boulder. Pick up the oar. Dragging one oar and manipulating the other, you are still heading into that boulder. Try something different. In your mind, find another way around that boulder. Even if you crash into a boulder, just push yourself away and keep going.

Relax. You're going to make it. When you are ready, begin to row again. You may crash into a boulder occasionally, but eventually, notice how you start to control the boat. While it seemed to be out of your control when you began this trip, you can now move it about in the river with ease. You may have noticed that you tired quickly when you first started rowing, but the more you row, the easier it becomes. Your muscles are becoming accustomed to the rowing movement, just as your muscles are becoming used to walking in the woods.

You may even begin to notice a warm sensation in your muscles. Your muscles are working for you even when you decide to relax. Like the river rolling along daily, you are becoming more capable each day of handling obstacles and challenges in your life. Take a deep breath and let any frustrations and concerns roll away like the water's current. Let it go.

Notice the strength of the water as it hits a boulder standing in its way. Imagine that strength building up in you. Each day you are becoming stronger and more resistant to obstacles. You made it yesterday. Today you have even more strength and stamina working for you. Imagine you will make it today. Imagine your body will work for you as easily as it breathes for you. With no thought. It just happens.

Notice your reflection in the river. The reflection is the person you are preparing to become. Imagine how this reflection will handle obstacles in the future. Can you think of a problem or a time when you reacted by letting the stress build up in your body? Now imagine three ways you can handle problems without creating stress? What can you do instead? Once you have all three solutions, put them in your backpack for future use. Take them out any time you need them, without hesitation.

Look at your reflection again, and see yourself resolving a problem. What is the problem? How do you look, how do you feel right now? What are you saying to yourself? Put your hand into the river and swirl your reflection around until you can't make it out anymore.

Now visualize the same problem, but this time, pull one of the solutions from your backpack. How will this solution work? How do you look using this solution? How does it feel? What are you saying to yourself this time? If you are happy with this solution, return it to your backpack for future use. If you're not happy with it, toss it into the river.

Try your other solutions. How does each solution look when you're using it on a problem? How does it feel? What are you saying to yourself? If you are happy with this solution, keep it. Otherwise, toss it into the river.

If you have two comfortable solutions, you are ready to move on. If you do not have suitable solutions stop right here and make a list of other options that are available to you. Visualize each option and how it feels. Make sure you are happy with the options. If you are not sure, try your options out for several days to see how it works and how it feels. You can always come back to this segment if you need more options.

Continue rowing along the river. Begin counting from one, up to two. You may be feeling eager to continue rowing, so let no one stop you. Three and four, notice that as you row your awareness of the room surrounding you is blending into the river and the woods. Five and six, your breathing is quicker. Seven and eight you are preparing to leave the river, but your subconscious is still working, searching for suitable solutions as you hear nine and ten. When you are ready, try your solutions out in reality.

Chapter Eight

Achieving Stronger Relationships with Visualization

It happened at 8:30 every morning. The young couple living next door to me began their morning ritual, an argument. Only once in three years was there a break from the fighting; she was in the hospital recovering from a fight that had led to a beating. Although the couple did seek counseling and stay together, it became apparent that neither was willing to change enough to improve their marriage, and the arguments continued. The sad thing about this couple is that if they can't make the changes necessary to improve their marriage, they'll have fifty or sixty years of unhappiness together.

Unlike this young couple, most of us need only minor adjustments to improve our relationships. However, even minor changes can be difficult because we have to take the time to look at, and change ourselves. The purpose of this chapter is to teach you visualization techniques that can enhance your relationships by helping you change what you are doing. Since you are the one reading the book, you are the only person who can be expected to change. Visualization works, but first you need to determine what to visualize. We're going to begin by helping you determine where you are in your relationships.

Think of a relationship you want to enhance and check the areas that apply to you:

_____**The relationship is sometimes turbulent. There is occasional resentment and hostility.**

Correcting Thoughts

Expressing the reasons for these thoughts can help the partners decide what to. For example, you may be angry. It will be best to diffuse your thoughts before approaching your partner. Take a moment to write out your thoughts, but instead of blaming your partner, or making your partner wrong, focus on the behavior you're angry about, and how that behavior makes you feel. Instead of writing, "You were wrong for coming home late," you could begin with "I feel angry when I have to wait for you. It makes me feel that you don't value me and my time. Would you be willing to work with me until we find a solution that is comfortable for both of us?"

Correcting Behaviors

What behaviors will work best in approaching your partner? Consider the tone of voice you'll use: harsh or softened? Should you talk in a slow pace, or fast? Imagine listening to your partner's needs and taking the time to discover how you might fulfill that need.

Imagine discussing your needs. How will you react if your partner gets defensive or angry? Can you imagine remaining calm, not getting stubborn, or defensive, or angry? Can you imagine a conversation with no threats? Can you imagine a conversation that allows each person involved to retain his or her dignity, even if you vehemently disagree with each other? List one behavior you want to work on today.

Visualization Solution

Once you are comfortable, imagine approaching your partner in an adult manner. Being adult means you are open to listening, to speaking, and to finding a solution that makes all involved parties comfortable. Once you are in this state of mind, take a moment to relax. Begin visualizing how you will approach your partner. When will you approach your partner, where will you talk, where will you sit, or stand? Imagine saying the words you have written in a calm tone of voice. Picture sitting or standing in a relaxed position. Visualize the scene and working with your partner to find a solution you are both comfortable with (use brainstorming techniques to discover your options). If the conversation gets tense, if someone starts to place blame, to criticize, to scream, to become stubborn, or to demand they get their own way, imagine taking a break. Return to the discussion once everyone is calm and coming from an adult frame of mind.

_____**If you are feeling dislike toward your partner, focusing on the positive side of your partner and the value of the relationship can help.**

Correcting Thoughts

Begin by making a list of what attracted you to your partner in the first place:

1
2
3
4
5

Next, list everything you value about the relationship:

1
2
3
4
5

Correcting Behaviors

What behavior(s) can you use today, and for the remainder of this week, to make each day better for your partner?

1
2
3
4
5

How can you meet your partner's needs today?

1
2
3
4
5

Visualization Solution

Take a moment to relax and think about the positive aspects of your partner. How do these thoughts make you feel?

Imagine being excited at the prospect of being with your partner, today. Remember how good it felt to be with this person when you first met? Imagine that feeling. Remember the anticipation and excitement you felt? Feel it again. You can experience this feeling anytime you choose. You control your emotions. Choose to enjoy your partner.

Take five minutes each day to relax and remember what you value in this relationship.

Focus on the positive aspects of the relationship, what it brings you, and how much you enjoy being involved with your partner.

Tip: ***Your thoughts and behaviors create your reality***

Creating Fulfilling Relationships

While many of us intuitively know what it takes to achieve fulfilling relationships, the divorce rate indicates that more than half of us are incapable of applying that knowledge. Of the couples that remain married, conservative estimates reveal that only one in 10 is happy; it is more likely that only one in 25 is truly happy.

So, what makes us truly happy? Having our emotional needs, psychological needs and physical needs met maximizes our happiness. Our partner's purpose then, is to help us maximize that happiness.

Emotional needs are met when we can communicate our feelings and desires. Communication has two aspects: talking and listening. Give each other equal time to both talk and listen.

How could you maximize your partner's emotional needs? (Tip: ask your partner).

1)
2)
3)

Psychological needs include being honest with your partner; being dependable, doing what you say you will do; having fun with your partner; being forgiving, patient, and not infringing upon your partner's freedom. Freedom is allowing your partner the space to be who he or she is, the time to pursue his or her own interests. The more you try to limit another's interest and insist all their time be spent with you, the more you try to control and possess another, the less you both enjoy the relationship. No one wants to feel owned. If you manage to control another person, you may have a relationship that lasts forever, but it is not a loving or fulfilling relationship. Loving and fulfilling relationships help each other grow and fulfill their own purpose for being here on earth.

How could you maximize your partner's psychological needs? (Tip: ask your partner).

1)
2)
3)

Physical needs include affection, holding, touching, hugging, and in an intimate relationship, sex and romance. Fulfilling these needs maximizes our happiness.

How could you maximize your partner's physical needs? (Tip: ask your partner).

1)
2)
3)

When we feel good about ourselves in the context of the relationship, we are happier. But how often do you feel happy when another person tries to make you feel wrong. Deterioration in relationships often begins with the need to make the other person wrong, or yourself right. To be right, you have to win the argument, you have to be superior. I don't know too many of us who feel happy or fulfilled when we feel inferior. We all have a need to feel good about ourselves and we need to honor that space in others too. Honoring this space doesn't mean you have to agree with everything someone else believes. If you disagree you could respond with, "I see that a different way." You might even get a chance to explain how you see things differently if the other person is interested and asks for your opinion. When we share opinions and discover the options that are available to us, the conversation is exhilarating ... we learn and grow by exchanging ideas with others. But the moment you offer another person advice, or imply that your solution is the correct way, the implication is that the other person is too stupid to find a solution on their own. The conversation is shut down.

How can you honor your partner's ideas and dreams without offering advice, or implying you have a better solution?

1)
2)
3)

Take a moment right now and write down five ways that you can make a day better for your partner. Do at least one item from your list each day.

1)

2)

3)

4)

5)

Enduring Relationships

Perhaps you can make a day better for your partner by reviewing a study from Purdue University. This study found that enduring relationships have the following components:

_____Partners can resolve differences of opinion with ease.

_____Partners can express feelings of emotional closeness.

_____Partners are committed to the relationship.

_____Partners build self-confidence and self-esteem in each other.

_____Partners can play and work together comfortably.

_____Partners respond desirably toward each other, irrespective of content.

_____(If the partners are intimate) sexual needs are communicated and fulfilled by the relationship (Norton).

These findings are still relevant today. Check the areas above that you want to strengthen. Relationships should feel good. "Feeling good" is an accurate measure of when to remain involved in a relationship. If the relationship doesn't "feel good," something needs adjusting. And adjusting starts with you, not your partner! If you don't like the results you're getting, send out a new message. We all deserve to be treated with love and respect. If a desirable end for everyone involved in the relationship cannot be found, perhaps it is time to seek counseling. Asking for a third party intervention is not a failure. It simply means people are having difficulty finding solutions on their own. Counselors can offer new options that have not been considered previously. Life does not have to be a struggle unless we envision it that way. Relationships do not have to be a continuous struggle, either, unless you stay in a relationship that is a struggle and do nothing to change its status. The choice is yours.

Most of us think about primary relationships when we talk about relationships, but the same ingredients that make a marriage effective, also make relationships with family, friends, and co-workers more effective.

Having good relationships is something most of us want, and need. Studies show that happily married men have superior mental health, lower suicide rates, greater career prospects, and longer lives. This makes sense when you consider that when we're happy, we experience less stress, lower rates of alcohol and substance abuse, and better health.

In other words, good relationships make us feel good psychologically, physically, and emotionally, despite that we have differences and dislikable qualities. If we're feeling bad, something needs to be changed. The only things that change are things each individual wants to change. If you want to become more affectionate, visualizing yourself as more affectionate can help you achieve it!

Notice that the focus of this chapter is on you, not your partner. Since you are the person reading this book, you are the only person expected to change. Any change you make will affect your relationships too, eventually.

I have a friend who refuses to be on time for any event, which drives me crazy. When I first met Wilda if she was late I would wait for her, and then I'd be angry when she arrived. She would end up angry too, because I was fussing at her. Finally, we agreed that if she was late again, I would go on without her. Her behavior does not have an effect on what I'm doing, anymore. And I'm not trying to change her behaviors. I just accept her. Has this change in our behaviors changed our relationship? Yes. We get along better, and neither of us is angry anymore. We have found a way to relate with each other that works for both of us, we simply accept each other.

What specific changes will you make to feel better in your relationships? List the items you checked earlier, plus anything else that comes to mind.

Relationship Log

1)
2)
3)
4)
5)

Place a star by the two items on your relationship log that are most important for you to achieve. Then list any specific times you are prone to have problems in this area. For example, Jill loses her temper easily when she is tired. Although she takes precautions against overworking and overplaying, there are times she goes beyond her "tired threshold." "I take it as my responsibility to warn my partner that I'm tired and becoming short-tempered. With this warning, he understands that there are some topics that would be better discussed at a later date. If I do get upset about something that he believes is insignificant, he can pass it off as, "she's tired, I'm not going to get into an argument with her." In addition, if he forgets my warning, I can remind him, "I'm tired, can we discuss this tomorrow?" When we can take a good look at ourselves, when we understand our strengths and weaknesses, we become better at giving and getting emotional fulfillment.

It's what you learn about relationships after you think you know it all that really counts!

Leo Buscaglia

Visualization Script For Fulfilling Relationships

Take a moment to relax and think for a moment, how is it possible to create a fulfilling relationship? Think about one of the items you checked above. While you are thinking, begin counting from 10 down to one. With each number allow yourself to relax more and more. Ten, what will keep you from acting the way you desire? What will keep you from a loving relationship? Nine, relax and think about this for a moment. Allow the muscles in your feet and ankles to begin relaxing, can you feel it? Just allow it to happen. Eight, we are most comfortable doing things the way we always have. Until you have the opportunity to practice the behavior you desire of yourself, it may seem difficult, or as easy as making the muscles in your lower calves begin to relax. Seven, imagine a warm feeling moving up your legs and relaxing the muscles as you read. As the warmth goes over your knees, the thigh muscles become relaxed. Six, you are making the choice to relax more and more. For a few minutes, you are going to have the opportunity to look into your future and practice becoming the person you desire, you will practice creating fulfilling relationships. Five, the more you believe you are capable of becoming the person you desire, the more you will begin to act in a way consistent with achieving your desires.

Four, you are capable of allowing a warm feeling to slither into your lower abdominal. Notice the control you have over relaxing these muscles. Allow the warmth and relaxation to deepen as it moves into your chest and along your arms. Three, have you noticed that each time you exhale you are becoming more and more comfortable and relaxed? Perhaps you've noticed the need to take a deeper breath now. Two, allow the muscles all the way down to your fingertips to feel like a limp, wet rag. Allow the warmth to move across your shoulders, into your neck and lower jaw, and then across your check-bones. Feel the muscles around your eyes and across your forehead relaxing.   One, as the relaxation moves over your head, your entire body feels more comfortable, and more relaxed.

What is one area you are working on today? What will it take for you to achieve it? Imagine you have a guide helping you take one step at a time toward achieving the relationship you desire. You cannot see this guide, but if you listen, you will receive the answers you need. Perhaps there is more than one answer; perhaps there is more than one guide. Write down what comes to your mind, listen to your guide, follow the instructions.

Have you ever had the feeling that someone is watching over you? Someone is watching you right now. Imagine it! Every move is being observed by an invisible energy. It surrounds you. Tap into its energy; it is always there for you, on any decision, if you choose to listen. When you are upset, angry, or frustrated in your relationships, your guide is willing to help; when you are happy, when you have to make a decision, or when you wonder if you have made the right decision, your guide is there. You are not alone in this universe. Allow your guide to direct you along the correct path. Relax and just listen to your inner guide.

If you believe you can achieve fulfilling relationships, if you believe you can be happy in your relationships, you can! It begins with your thoughts. What do you want and need to make your relationship more fulfilling, today? What does your partner want and need? How can you help your partner achieve happiness and fulfillment?

Focus on one thought; imagine making one change in how you will relate in your relationships today? What is that one change? Imagine you will begin creating this change the moment you finish reading this chapter. The change begins with you. What will you do differently?

Are you concerned with how others will react to your change? Visualize not being concerned with how others will respond. Relax. Be concerned with giving love and respect. Follow your guide. Believe that everything will turn out for the best.

As you continue throughout this day, imagine that everyone you encounter needs you, and that you have something wonderful to offer them. How do you want to relate to people the remainder of this day? How will you relate to someone who is angry? Can you imagine just sitting in silence, or calmly removing yourself from the scene if someone is angry? Or sending out love, instead? How will you relate to someone who is demanding, or sad? You are responsible for your own thoughts and behaviors.

Visualize your relationships as you choose them to be. Work on yourself. Imagine a new way of reacting to a situation, then behave in that fashion. You cannot make others behave as you think they should, but you can behave in the way you think you should. Circumstances do not control how you behave. You control how you behave, despite your circumstances.

Relax knowing that you can achieve whatever you desire. Begin counting from one up to ten and with each number, experience an excitement about creating a new reality for yourself, and for your relationships.

One, for today try one new idea, or one new behavior to make your relationships better. Two, imagine using this new behavior. Three, imagine the reaction of those around you when you use this behavior. Are you getting the response you desired? Four, even if your relationship partner reacts in an old-way, imagine feeling good that you have made a positive correction in your behavior. Five, you are responsible for your emotions. Six, prepare to enter reality and try your new behavior. Seven, eight, nine and ten.

Relationship Maintenance

Each day read the visualization script again, and focus on one behavior you will use to enhance your relationships for that day only. Eventually, you will have the script memorized, and you will have formed new habits that focus on positive ways to create fulfilling relationships.

Chapter Nine

Design Your Own Visualizations

I f you have the misguided notion that visualization is like dreaming, think again! Visualization is not creating an imaginary world, or creating a vision of how the world might be. It is developing a script, a map, a detailed plan to help you achieve your goal. By following this plan you actually create the life you desire.

What do you want? Wealth, good fortune, fabulous looks? Whatever you want can be achieved only if you imagine that you already have it. For today, think as if you have already attained what you desire. Your desires begin with a thought. So think for a moment, what is one thing you can do today to accomplish your desire?

If you want a higher income, what steps can you take today to achieve a higher income? If you want a toned body, for today, think and behave like someone who has a toned body.

Positive thoughts create positive actions. Take one day at a time. For today, exercise like a person with a toned body, eat like this person, literally become this person for the day. Then do it again each day from this day forth.

Please fill out the contract below before you continue reading.

The Contract

I will work through the visualization exercises until I am clear about the thoughts and behaviors I desire:

The thought I wish to work on:

The behavior I wish to work on:

I am willing to work and continue using visualization until I reach my desired outcome

I will not give up on myself.

If I mess up today, I will begin my program again tomorrow!

Signed:

Date:

Each day visualize what thoughts, behaviors and specific action it will take to achieve your desired outcome. For example,

- What is something you want to change (current problem)?

- What is the outcome you desire?

- What thoughts must change for you to achieve this outcome (what negative thoughts or objections are holding you back?) For each negative thought, list two positive reasons for going after your goal anyway.

- What behavior must change for you to achieve this outcome?

- What specific steps must take place for you to achieve this outcome?

- On a daily basis, what is your plan?

- By what date do you wish to achieve this goal?

In case you haven't noticed, visualization has a measurable quality to it. It states exactly what you plan to do to accomplish your goal. Mary Lou Retton mind-scripted every move she would make at the Olympics; all she had to do was follow the plan. If you want to lose weight, it takes more than just stating " I want to lose weight," it takes following a plan: "Tomorrow I'll have orange juice and one egg for breakfast," imagine yourself doing this. "For lunch I'll eat a beef patty and cottage cheese." Once your day is planned, visualize going through the day as it is scripted. There will be no doubt if you have accomplished your goal. You can measure your success by what you actually did. If you make a mistake, adjust the visualization and begin again the next day.

Developing a Visualization

In this step, you will create a story to develop the desired thoughts, behaviors, and specific steps needed to achieve your goal. Think of someone who has succeeded at your endeavor. What is their story? If you don't know someone who has succeeded at the endeavor you desire, make up a story with the ending that you desire.

Think of it as being a character in a movie. As the first scene begins, you are reading this page. Who are the other characters in this movie? Are they with you right now, or do they enter later in the movie?

What needs to happen in this movie for your character to achieve the desired outcome? If you were to look at one day in the life of your character, what action must be taken today toward achieving your goal? Imagine this one-day as a scene in your movie. What thoughts must be present right now for you to begin working on your goal? What behavior needs to take place each hour of the day for you to achieve your outcome? What does your character look like moving about in this scene? Imagine this scene takes place in the morning. Where is your character going? What obstacles might get in your character's way? How does your character handle the obstacle?

Now look at the afternoon and develop your script, your thoughts, behaviors and actions that must take place before the evening arrives.

Now look at the evening hours and what must take place to achieve your goals.

For example, let's say you want to eliminate one cigarette today. You decide the 3 p.m. break at work is the time to eliminate this cigarette.

Step One: Develop a story watching yourself at 3 p.m. What will you do instead of smoke? Perhaps you'll go for a walk. Now, instead of simply watching yourself, imagine you are the star of the movie. Feel yourself taking a walk. Feel yourself leave the building for a ten-minute walk. Where will you walk? Imagine your walk in detail as if you are actually taking the walk. What stores will you pass? How will you feel walking? How will you look? Will you walk alone or with a partner? Imagine passing other people on the walk. Imagine a feeling of success and accomplishment once you have eliminated the 3 p.m. cigarette by walking.

Step Two: Next, imagine an obstacle getting in your way. How will you overcome the obstacle? Is the obstacle a person, a place, an animal, or something else? Using the stop smoking scenario, imagine you return to work and a friend offers you a cigarette. Imagine one option for overcoming this obstacle. For example: you could imagine yourself simply saying "No, thank you" and walking away.

What are your obstacles? Write out the solutions to overcoming each one.

Step Three: Imagine you are filming the movie now. You are leaving work at 3 p.m. to go for your walk, when a friend asks if you want to have a cigarette you simply say "no" and walk away. How does it feel using this option? What do you sound like using this option? What do you look like? Imagine the scene in great detail. Imagine what you will do and what you will say. Imagine going through each scene until the outcome is successfully achieved for that day.

Step Four: Actually try out the option you described above. If this option does not work, find another option and visualize using it. Keep repeating this step until you find an option that is successful. Maybe you'll find several options that work. Then pick the option that you like best and imagine using it when an obstacle gets in your way.

Step Five: Each day is another scene in your movie. Visualize moving through your entire day. Imagine what must be accomplished today, how will you think, how will you act? Imagine successfully accomplishing each day's goals. You have made a promise to yourself. Now keep it!

Each night before retiring for the evening, or at any convenient time, take ten minutes to relax and visualize your daily plan.

Getting What You Desire

Whatever you desire can be accomplished only if you believe you can achieve it. If someone else can achieve it, you can too. However, don't be too hard on yourself if at first you don't succeed. It takes practice to get to a level of competent communication with yourself and others. Once you reach this level of competent communication, whatever you are trying to achieve will seem natural. It's this natural level you are trying to achieve, where you no longer have to think about what you are doing.

If you are reading this book, you're probably not at the natural level yet. You are probably aware of the fact that something must change, but you may not be sure what to change. Think about what you have been doing, then do something different.

I used to go grocery shopping between breakfast and lunch, and it never failed, I was always hungry when I arrived at the store. And I always bought impulse items because I was hungry. Now, I do something different, I treat myself to a hamburger, fries, and milk shake before I shop. It keeps me from buying junk and impulse foods, which means I have no junk food in my house for the entire week. If I really want junk food, I have to make a special trip to get it, and usually I just don't want it that badly to make the special trip.

This same process worked when I quit smoking. I would buy one package of cigarettes instead of a carton. I stayed away from places where I enjoyed having a cigarette, like the break room at work, and I stopped socializing with the smokers. And anytime the thought came to my mind, "I can't quit smoking," I found two other reasons to continue toward my goal. "Yes, I can quit! I not going to stop until I get what I desire."

If what you are doing is not working, change it! Stop rationalizing why you can't change things and decide to just do it! If other people can do it, so can you!

Having worked through this book, you have acquired learning tools to help you achieve whatever you desire in your life. In the future, when you encounter problems, revisit these pages as guidance. You have the answer to every problem, concern, dream and desire within you. Following the spirit of your own mind is essential. Start visualizing it!

Conclusion

Tap Into Your Spiritual Self

T apping into your spiritual self has nothing to do with your religious beliefs. While your spiritual belief system may be called in God, Buddha, or another higher intelligence, visualization helps you tap into the power of your mind. It taps into the part of your mind that unconsciously knows how to achieve its desires, your spiritual self.

If you understand the concepts of this book, you realize that you are the only person you can change. I hope you also understand that you are the one who determines what kind of results you are going to have. This is the spirit we are individually following.

Many people use the argument "If God wanted me to achieve my dreams, I'd have them already." If this is your belief system, you might consider that God gave you all the ingredients to achieve your dreams: you have a mind to individually think with, you have innate desires, you have individual desires, and you have creative abilities. And God allows us the freedom to use these ingredients as we please.

Somehow, I doubt that an all giving and caring God is watching over us and deciding if you will win in Vegas, or go home broke; or which cars should bump into each other on the highways, or if you get a promotion or get fired. It's more likely an all giving God would give us the power to work these details out by ourselves, but would also be there as a guide if you choose to listen.

An interesting phenomenon occurs when you learn to tap into that guide and listen to your spiritual self. There is a calmness, your body quits fighting the suggestions your mind visualizes; there is an instinctive knowing that you are following the right path when you act on this information. The relaxation component in visualization helps you accomplish this.

Progressive relaxation not only relaxes the body, but it also relaxes the mind. It allows you to get rid of the unnecessary confusion and to get focused for action. You are learning to consult your mind before acting. You're making mental images a part of your daily routine. You're beginning to live by the images you design, to act upon the images in order to achieve your desires. To accomplish this, take ten minutes each day to visualize yourself actually accomplishing your desires, and banishing the boundaries that get in your way.

The only things you have to lose by trying visualization are unwanted thoughts and behaviors. I am suggesting that if there is something you desire, and any other person has accomplished it, you can accomplish it too. You can learn what thoughts and behaviors to practice, both mentally and in reality. It begins with you believing that it can happen.

Let's assume you can get the mental image you desire, but you have trouble eliminating negative thoughts and actually following through with correct behaviors. This is a common problem. Negative emotional reactions more often than not direct our decisions and outcomes rather than logical thinking does.

You might consider thinking of your mind as if it were your favorite cake. You can picture how the cake will look when it's finished baking, but you're having trouble deciding on the ingredients that go into the cake, and what amount to mix in. This common problem has an easy solution. If you want the cake to turn out, you find someone with a recipe, a list of ingredients and the exact amount of each ingredient, and you put them in exactly as the recipe calls for them. Then, you heat the oven, and let the recipe work its miracle in the time allotted.

Putting thoughts into our minds is a lot like baking. We are all capable of purchasing the same ingredients from the grocery store, but what we individually do with those ingredients, and how much of each ingredient we use, will produce different results. With the same ingredients in differing amounts you can create muffins, pancakes, cakes, and breads. From exactly the same ingredients, in differing amounts, your neighbor has created an entirely different dish, and tasting not one bit like your cake; and – this is the point – you knew you would get different results! That is why you choose these ingredients. Like baking, you need to select thoughts that will create the behaviors you want.

Most of us can't explain exactly how we get different results from the same ingredients, but I can guarantee you, if my grandmother made her Italian spaghetti sauce, and I used the exact ingredients, in the exact amounts, somehow mine never tasted the same as grandma's. But despite our lack of understanding, and these slight differences in the outcome, we continue to cook and eat. No one can explain why visualization works, either. But if we begin by practicing the correct thoughts, and eliminating negative ones, our minds will have the opportunity to produce the correct behaviors. Your outcome may not be exactly like someone else's, but it will be similar. Since you are the one who decides what ingredients to include in your mind, you personally then, are the one who determines what kind of results you are going to have.

The power is within you to set boundaries, or to banish any unrealistic boundaries that create limitations in your life. If a negative thought sneaks in, immediately think of two positive thoughts to counteract it. If you add a wrong behavior to the mix, change it! Try something different the next time. And keep trying something different until you get the outcome you desire.

Final Thoughts

If you are not willing to try something different, you have no right to complain about your circumstances. This is your journey. It begins today, but it is never ending. Working the plan is not meant to be sporadic. It means being committed to the long-term result and not giving up on yourself until you get what you are after.

Many people give up after a small setback, or an ill word, or rejection. I hear people lament all the time, "Do you think I choose to smoke?" Nobody else puts that cigarette in your mouth! "Do you think I choose to be fat?" Nobody else puts that food in your mouth! "Do you think I choose to be poor?" Nobody is making you stay in your current job! If you are not happy with your circumstances, only you can choose differently. Create a new way to communicate with yourself and others, create new visions to follow. Be one of those people who persist and achieve.

Today, I can tell you I want this book to get published. I believe I have something of value for my audience. If I weren't convinced I could help people, I wouldn't sit at my computer day after day for hours at a time, writing. I am not stopping! I can see this book getting published, I know how it will feel when it happens, I can see myself on book signing circuit, I can see myself doing talk shows, I want this to happen in my heart and soul. It is the most motivating and exhilarating feeling to work toward a desire. And as long as I don't quit, I believe it will happen. I tell myself it will happen and I visualize it happening. The techniques in this book have worked for me, and for others, and they can work for you too, but only if you continue to use them.

If you want to create a mindset for success, follow the techniques offered in this book. You can develop the thoughts, behaviors, and actions necessary to achieve the life you desire.

Many people are under the false impression that if you simply imagine what you want, you miraculously get it with visualization. This could not be further from the truth. Visualization is a specific strategy, with specific steps that need to be practiced in order to attain goals. Even if you have failed in the past, you are being programmed for success, today!

Get rid of negative thoughts. What thoughts immediately come to your mind when you think of your goal? What are you saying to yourself? If you have negative thoughts, they must be changed to positive thoughts for a successful performance. Most people I've worked with have a litany of negative thoughts that they are initially unaware of.

Knowing exactly what to imagine is important. The desired behaviors should be mentally practiced in a step-by-step, specific fashion for a minimum of ten minutes each day. If you imagine inaccurate behaviors, you'll get inaccurate results.

Be "associated." To be associated, you want to imagine you are actually performing the task; feel yourself doing the task. Disassociated is like watching yourself perform the task, as if you were watching a movie.

By correctly practicing the communication and visualization techniques offered in this book, you can turn negative internal thoughts and behaviors into positive ones, and **you can enhance the effectiveness of your efforts by 20% - 25%.** Correct thoughts equal correct behaviors, which equals the formula for success.

Steps To Visualization
Relax
Rid of negative thoughts
Correct behaviors
Develop a step-by step action plan and follow it
Be Associated

END

Works Cited

Bouchard, T.J. , (1972). Training, motivation, and personality as Determinants of effectiveness of brainstorming groups and individuals. Journal of Applied Psychology, 56, 324-331.

Dunnette, M.D., Campbell, J., & Jaastad, K. (1963). The effects of group participation on brainstorming effectiveness for two industrial samples. Journal of Applied Psychology, 47, 30-37.

Hirokawa, R.Y. (1982). Consensus group decision making, quality of decision, and group satisfaction: An attempt to sort fact from fiction. Central States Speech Journal, 33, 407-415.

Hirokawa, R.Y., & Pace, R.A. (1983). Descriptive investigation of the possible communication based reasons for effective and ineffective group decision making. Communication Monographs, 50, 362-381.

Hirokawa, R.Y. (1985). Discussion of procedures and decision making performance: test of a functional perspective. Human Communication Research, 12, 203-224.

McGarvey, Robert. Rehearsing for Success: Tap the power of the mind through visualization. Executive Female, Jan. , 1990, 35.

Norton, R. (1983). Measuring Marital Quality: A critical look at dependant variables. Journal of Marriage and Family, 45, 141-151.

Osborn, A.F. (1957). Applied Imagination. New York: Scribner.

Rasco, R.W., Tennyson, R.D., & Boutwell, R.C. (1975). Imagery instructions and drawings in learning prose. Journal of Educational Psychology, 67, 2, 188-192.

Ruback, B., Dabbs, J., & Hopper, C. (1984). The process of brainstorming: An analysis with individual and group vocal parameters. Journal of Personality and Social Psychology, 47, 558-567.

Ryans, E.D., & Simons, J. (1982)). Efficacy of mental imagery in enhancing mental rehearsal of motor skills. Journal of Sport Psychology, 4, 41-51.

Wells, S.F., (1962). Improve your swing without swinging. Golf Digest, 13, 24-28.

Also by the author:

Professional Seminars

(Conducted on /off cite. Programs are designed to support your goals).

Speak and Get More Business
> *Learn to captivate your audience, engage your clients, and make your business become predictable!*

Persuasive Techniques That Never Fail!
> *Gain a competitive edge, develop an in-depth knowledge of how to effectively work with others, manage others, and inspire others.*

Create Visions That Others Will Act Upon With Enthusiasm
> *Take your business to a higher level. Exceed your goals. Build infectious excitement to help your staff work at their peak.*

Personal Growth Home Workshops

Lose Weight with Visualization Home Workshop $29.95
> *Workbook and cassette tape series*

Reduce Stress with Visualization Home Workshop $29.95
> *Workbook and cassette tape series*

Stop Smoking with Visualization Home Workshop $29.95
> *Workbook and cassette tape series*

Speaking Series

"If At First You Don't Succeed, Try Something Different."
"Making Work Something Other Than a Four-Letter Word"
"Typical Thoughts, Triumphant Results!"

CD and Tapes are coming soon! For more information contact:
F.A.C.T. Publication @ (770) 579-2577, email: F.A.C.T.S@att.net
or use the order form on the following page.

To Order : Books, Tapes or Home Workshops
or to inquire about professional seminars & speeches

Call:	**(770) 579-2577**
Fax orders:	**(770) 579-2577/ Send this form.**
email orders:	**F.A.C.T.S@att.net**
Postal orders:	**F.A.C.T.**
	P.O. Box 6124
	Marietta, Ga 30062

Please send the following books, workbooks or tapes.
I may return any of them for a full refund no questions asked, please call
(770) 579-2577 for a return authorization number.

Typical Thoughts, Triumphant Results $14.95

_____

_____

Please send free information on:
Other books   Speaking/Seminars   Mailing Lists   Consulting

Name: _____
Address: _____
City: _____ State _____ Zip _____

Telephone: _____
e:mail _____

Program Cost:
Home Workshop cost:
Book cost: _____
Shipping ($3.95 for the first item   _____
and $2.00 for each additional item)
Sales Tax
Total Amount   _____

                                         _____

Payment: Check   Credit Card: Visa/Mastercard
Card number: _____

Name on card: _____

Exp. Date: _____

To Order :   Books, Tapes or Home Workshops
or to inquire about professional seminars & speeches

Call: (770) 579-2577
Fax orders: (770) 579-2577/ Send this form.
email orders: F.A.C.T.S@att.net
Postal orders: F.A.C.T.
                     P.O. Box 6124
                     Marietta, Ga 30062

Please send the following books, workbooks or tapes.
I may return any of them for a full refund no questions asked, please call
(770) 579-2577 for a return authorization number.

Typical Thoughts, Triumphant Results   **$14.95**

_____

_____

Please send free information on:
Other books   Speaking/Seminars   Mailing Lists   Consulting

Name: —————————————————————————
Address: ————————————————————————
City: ——————————— State ———— Zip ————

Telephone: ——————————————————————
e-mail:
        ———————————————————————————

Program cost:
Home Workshop cost:
Book cost: ——————————
Shipping ($3.95 for the first item
and $2.00 for each additional item)
Sales Tax   ——————————
Total Amount   ——————————

Payment: Check   Credit Card: Visa/Mastercard
Card number: ——————————————————————

Name on card: —————————————————————

Exp. Date: ———————————————